Perhaps the most playful, informative, and easily digestible book on becomi
The thorough list of tips a
for psychologists—wheth
ence presentations, perfe
cating effectively to the
statistical significance means nothing). This book is superb because these two authors are extremely entertaining and they know how to make ideas stick.

—*Todd B. Kashdan, PhD, Professor of Psychology, George Mason University, Fairfax, VA, and author of* Curious? Discover the Missing Ingredient to a Fulfilling Life.

Whether facing a conference presentation, job talk, or speech to the lay public, both new and seasoned academics will benefit from Feldman and Silvia's lighthearted yet practical advice on public speaking. On topics ranging from knowing your audience to preparing good PowerPoint slides to managing anxiety, this book offers solutions to common speaker woes and highlights the pleasures of successfully communicating theory and research to others.

—*Monica Biernat, PhD, Professor of Psychology, University of Kansas, Lawrence*

This book provides a realistic and humorous approach to the nuanced details of preparing talks. The authors do a wonderful job of making explicit and then masterfully defusing all the implicit fears that most speakers have. I recommend the book not only for graduate students and professionals who wish to improve their speaking but also for undergraduate psychology majors who are planning on attending graduate school.

—*Terri L. Bonebright, PhD, Chair and Professor of Psychology, DePauw University, Greencastle, IN*

Graduate students and undergraduates (and even seasoned presenters) who devote an afternoon to reading this engaging book will likely come away with specific ways to enhance their research talks. Time well spent!

—*Annette L. Stanton, PhD, Professor of Psychology and Psychiatry/Biobehavioral Sciences, University of California, Los Angeles*

This book is a must-read for students and early career psychologists at any experience level preparing for poster presentations, research discussions, or job talks. A valuable guide you'll want to reference before, during, and after your proposal is submitted.

—*Kenneth R. Liberatore, PhD, Co-Chair, Committee on Early Career Psychologists, California Psychological Association*

What a great resource for senior undergraduates, graduate students, and young professionals in psychology! Feldman and Silvia shed light on the overarching basics of effective professional communication and offer specific suggestions for various presentation formats. This little book is packed with practical advice, reassuring encouragement, and humorous examples that will help prepare novice presenters for forays into the important, and sometimes scary, world of professional speaking.

—*Jennifer S. Cheavens, PhD, Assistant Professor, Department of Psychology, The Ohio State University, Columbus*

PUBLIC SPEAKING
FOR
Psychologists

PUBLIC SPEAKING
FOR
Psychologists

**A Lighthearted Guide to
Research Presentations, Job Talks,
and Other Opportunities to
Embarrass Yourself**

DAVID B. FELDMAN *AND* **PAUL J. SILVIA**

American Psychological Association · *Washington, DC*

Published by
American Psychological Association
750 First Street, NE
Washington, DC 20002
www.apa.org

To order
APA Order Department
P.O. Box 92984
Washington, DC 20090-2984
Tel: (800) 374-2721; Direct: (202) 336-5510
Fax: (202) 336-5502; TDD/TTY: (202) 336-6123
Online: www.apa.org/books/
E-mail: order@apa.org

In the U.K., Europe, Africa, and the Middle East, copies may be ordered from
American Psychological Association
3 Henrietta Street
Covent Garden, London
WC2E 8LU England

Typeset in Minion and Goudy by Circle Graphics, Inc., Columbia, MD

Printer: Sheridan Books, Inc., Ann Arbor, MI
Cover Designer: Naylor Design, Washington, DC
Technical/Production Editor: Harriet Kaplan

The opinions and statements published are the responsibility of the authors, and such opinions and statements do not necessarily represent the policies of the American Psychological Association.

Library of Congress Cataloging-in-Publication Data
Feldman, David B.
  Public speaking for psychologists : a lighthearted guide to research presentations, job talks, and other opportunities to embarrass yourself / David B. Feldman and Paul J. Silvia.
      p. cm.
  Includes bibliographical references and index.
  ISBN-13: 978-1-4338-0730-5
  ISBN-10: 1-4338-0730-0
  ISBN-13: 978-1-4338-0731-2 (e-book)
  ISBN-10: 1-4338-0731-9 (e-book)
1. Public speaking. 2. Psychologists. I. Silvia, Paul J., 1976- II. Title.
  PN4192.P79F45 2010
  808.5'1—dc22
                                        2009031065

British Library Cataloguing-in-Publication Data
A CIP record is available from the British Library.

Printed in the United States of America
First Edition

Contents

Preface

Although human beings are by nature an optimistic lot, we view some events with dread. Near the top of most people's list of dreads—in between "koalas coming down from the eucalyptus trees and rising up against humanity" and "caffeine declared a controlled substance"—is "public speaking." Few people take naturally to talking in front of an audience. They don't look forward to it, they don't volunteer to do it, and they don't do it as well as they could. But a career in psychology and its kindred fields could involve a lot of public speaking, so you should learn to do it well. With time and practice, you can become a confident, effective presenter.

Effective public speaking involves learning a few rules and tricks, practicing at home, and then getting out and doing your best. In this book, we cover the basic principles that apply to all scholarly presentations and then consider some common genres, such as research talks, posters, job talks, and presentations to lay audiences. Although our book has an audience of beginners in mind—newly minted professionals, graduate students, and advanced undergraduates—we hope that even grizzled veterans of the conference world will find something useful here.

We wrote this book using the time-honored tactic of dividing the chapters between the authors, so astute readers will notice slightly different writing styles. If you're curious to know who wrote each chapter, simply look for coordinating adverbs (Dave), asyndetic coordination (Paul), and actual scholarly references (Dave) instead of mere opinion (Paul). Or you could look for who wrote the chapter's "Woeful Tale of Woe." The order of authorship was determined via a complex set of factors: height, love of Mexican telenovelas, household cat-to-dog ratio, level of caffeine addiction, number of Volvos owned, and amount pledged to National Public Radio over the past decade. Despite our differences on these dimensions, we share responsibility (i.e., blame each other) for the book's errors and flaws.

Many people helped with this book, and most of them didn't know it. Over the years, we've received good public-speaking advice from mentors, friends, and colleagues. The valiant students in our speaking-intensive courses deserve special thanks. And, of course, Linda McCarter, Emily Leonard, and the crew at APA Books deserve thanks for their help and work on this book. Editing and publishing is a craft unto itself, one unrecognized by readers but appreciated by authors.

I

GENERAL PRINCIPLES OF PUBLIC SPEAKING

1

Speaking (and Stammering) About Psychology

Children yearn to be like adults: They can't wait to grow up, to be big and independent, to be tall enough to reach the cabinets that store the dangerous stuff. As adults, these kids will feel ripped off. Much of adult life is a bleak morass of responsibility. We rationalize the hard stuff, the deliberate frustration and self-denial, by saying that it's good for us, that "it builds character." Only boring or painful things elevate our characters. Don't bother with riding horses, spending a Sunday eating bagels and drinking coffee, or hosting a Harry Potter movie binge. Instead, consider adopting a highway, reading *The Collected Works of Guy de Maupassant*, or volunteering to prepare injured koalas for their return to the wild.

Sometimes, the process of building character looks suspiciously like low-grade panic. We see this when we teach public speaking to our undergraduate and graduate students. The atmosphere turns sour on presentation days. The normally chatty students become quiet; the anxious students tap their feet like drummers in a speed-metal band; the presenter twists the laser pointer like it's an amulet that will forestall the looming End of Days. Despite their anxiety, we force our students to give presentations for two reasons. First, we are thwarted, nefarious people who find joy in others' suffering. Second, we believe that effective public speaking, like any skill, is learned through practice.

It's unfortunate that psychology's two ways of communicating—writing and public speaking—both can be painful. One day, we hope, gossiping over coffee will supplant research talks as psychology's prevailing mode of scholarly communication. But it won't happen soon, if only because it's hard to cite gossip in APA Style (cf. Feldman & Silvia, 2008). So we're stuck with writing and speaking. As a field, we're pretty poor at training people in these skills. Because a few lucky students have good writers and speakers as advisors, the mentorship model of graduate training sometimes works well. But many students are expected to learn these skills on the street, not in the classroom, and the public-speaking street is in a sketchy part of town.

Learning by doing, also known as *active learning* or *experiential learning*, has its virtues. But *observational learning*, also known as *saving-my-damn-time-by-hearing-about-that-fool's-embarrassing-mistakes*, is far more practical. Life is difficult enough without having to learn everything the hard, active way. During your stint preparing koalas for their return to the wild, for example,

4

your supervisor—a koala-rehabilitation expert—will probably say, "Don't poke that koala with a eucalyptus branch, mate." Consider your options. You could learn by making your own mistakes—once mauled by a feral koala, twice shy—or you could learn vicariously. "Okay, I won't poke that koala with a eucalyptus branch. Thanks for sharing that insight into marsupial behavior."

Over the years, you'll learn a lot about public speaking simply by doing it; some things can be learned only in the trenches, not in books. But sometimes book learning should precede street learning. Learning through mistakes is probably not the best idea for skills that require facing a group of people who are staring at you and waiting for you to say something interesting.

The purpose of this book is to introduce the basic principles of professional public speaking. Whether you plan to give a research talk, a poster, a job talk, or even a talk to the lay public, this book has some valuable rules, ideas, and tricks to offer. We presume that you're a beginner. Our primary imagined reader is someone in graduate school facing his or her first important presentation. You may have given some class presentations as an undergraduate; perhaps you've already given a poster at a conference. Even if you've had more or less experience than this, you'll improve by focusing on the fundamentals. If you're a grizzled public-speaking veteran, then you probably don't need this book; it's okay to put it down and get back to Guy de Maupassant.

We further presume that public speaking makes you nervous. Although you can learn to enjoy speaking to crowds, few beginners like it. You might be merely nervous: You don't like public speaking, but you can do it without a lot of drama. Some of you, however, may feel the talk looming over you: You ruminate about it beforehand, you feel agitated the day of the talk, you worry about how you did once the cursed thing is over. Some of you may even be anxious enough to see a specialist, such as a clinical psychologist, for treatment.

Some people, of course, enjoy public speaking; perhaps it doesn't bother you. Even if you're a natural, you still must hone your skills. Many naturally confident speakers, like many reality-TV contestants, don't know how foolish they look. Their confidence stems from egocentrism, not from skills developed through reading, practice, and experience. They could benefit from a measured dose of anxiety to motivate them to take the talk more seriously, consider their audience's perspective, and rehearse. (For what it's worth, Dave is a natural and Paul is simply unnatural.)

If public speaking arouses terror, you may have thought, "Can't I avoid this forever? I'll simply never apply to speak at a conference." You could, in principle, never give a professional presentation, but the costs could include restricted job options and a stunted career. Realistically, it's hard to avoid public speaking. In graduate school, your advisor will probably force you to present a poster or give a conference talk. When you look for employment, you'll find that all academic jobs and an occasional nonacademic research job will require you to give a presentation during the interview.

During your career, you may be invited to speak at conferences, conduct workshops, or even do media interviews. You can't say no to everything without looking like a scraggly-bearded hermit.

In our opinion, many books about public speaking have a naive view of anxiety. Psychology knows a lot about managing anxiety: We know what works for most people, what works for only some people, and what doesn't work despite sounding sensible. This book provides realistic advice for managing—not curing, conquering, or obliterating—your anxiety. You can make public speaking less nerve-wracking, but you can't cure anxiety simply by reading a book. For now, your goals are to learn the basics and do your best. Over time, old-fashioned exposure will conquer your anxiety for you.

This book is based on our experience as speakers and as teachers of public speaking. We've given most of the types of talks that academic psychologists give, such as posters, brief research talks, long research talks, job talks, panel discussions, invited colloquia, award addresses, clinical presentations, continuing-education seminars, media interviews, and workshops. We've also evaluated conference submissions, organized conferences, invited people to speak, served on search committees, and witnessed a near-infinite number of mind-numbing presentations.

The first half of the book covers the central skills of public speaking; the second half applies these skills to psychology's major genres. We recommend reading Chapters 2 through 6 in order. The tips in these chapters pertain to every kind of talk, so don't skimp on learning the fundamentals. The remaining chapters can be read pragmatically, depending on the kind of presentation you'll be giving. In each chapter, we share a "Woeful Tale of Woe," a character-building story of when we inadvertently poked the koala with a eucalyptus branch. We've made many mistakes and encountered many mishaps over the years. But we survived, and you can avoid making the same errors.

We start by discussing the importance of knowing your audience and viewing your talk from its perspective. Chapter 2 beats this idea into the ground, exhumes it with a backhoe, stabs a stake through its heart, and then beats it back into the ground. All presentations involve speaking to someone. This audience shapes the talk's scope, style, tone, and purpose, so you should begin by considering who will be listening.

In Chapter 3, we discuss the nuts and bolts of preparing and delivering a talk. We walk you through the basics of writing, practicing, revising, and delivering your presentation. Chapter 4 then describes how to answer the questions that will follow this talk. Conducting the Q&A session is a dark art of its own. What kind of questions should you expect? How can you handle weird and confusing questions? In Chapter 5, we turn to public-speaking anxiety. We take a realistic, empirical look at ways to manage feelings of anxiety before and during your talk. Chapter 6 ends the basic-skills section by considering tales of strife and disaster. What should you do if disaster strikes during your presentation? Many problems can be prevented; the rest can be handled with humor, grace, and fire extinguishers.

The remaining chapters cover psychology's four major speaking genres. Chapter 7 describes how to develop and present a research talk. We explain how to develop and give psychology's typical 15-minute conference presentation. This type of talk is great for beginners: if it goes badly, at least it was short. In addition, it's the foundation on which all other talks in the field of psychology are built. In Chapter 8, we turn to research posters. For most people, posters are their first conference presentations, and for good reason: They're relatively casual and easy, and few things can go wrong. If you want an academic job, you'll also be giving a lot of job talks. Because of the high stakes involved, you don't want to bungle these presentations. Chapter 9 offers advice gleaned from giving our own job talks, sitting through dozens of other people's job talks, and serving on faculty search committees. Chapter 10 describes how to talk to normal people, euphemistically known as *lay audiences* or *general audiences*. Normal people don't want to sit through a long talk packed with bulleted lists—this, we suppose, is the source of their normalcy. Because lay audiences are less masochistic than academic audiences, you'll need different strategies for these presentations.

Finally, our epilogue wraps up the book with some encouraging words and koala non sequiturs.

2

The First Commandment of Public Speaking: Know Thine Audience

If you believe that psychological research has been corrupted by greed and trendiness—the tendency to study whatever fads appeal to funding agencies—you'd enjoy hanging around your university's department of classical studies. These old school professors put things in perspective. Psychologists itch to discover the next big idea and to develop the next big theory; classicists know that any big idea was developed thousands of years ago, long before the invention of pants or forks. If you show them an exciting new study in the *Journal of Personality and Social Psychology*, they'll show you a Greek dramatist, a Jewish historian, or an Islamic mathematician who discovered it first.

Most of what we know about effective public speaking comes from the classical rhetorical tradition, particularly Aristotle's *Rhetoric*. Aristotle contended that features of the audience, along with the speaker's character and arguments, determined the presentation's persuasiveness. Aristotle's insistence on the importance of the audience was radical at the time. It sounds less radical thousands of years later—this is yet another reason why he is Aristotle and we are Dave and Paul. Nevertheless, this chapter describes why and how to take your audience's perspective when developing a presentation. To be effective, you must understand who will be listening to your talk.

Much of this chapter may sound obvious. But people often fail to follow ideas that can seem too simple to be true. People have known about the importance of the audience since Aristotle's time, but they rarely take his advice. Public-speaking novices are particularly likely to neglect their listeners: They can be too absorbed in their own anxiety to take the audience's perspective. As a result, some talks are pitched too high, over the audience's heads, and others are pitched too low, as if the speaker were reading *Good Night, Gorilla* to a roomful of toddlers. We'll thus review some modern tips for understanding your audience; for the classical perspective, consult Aristotle's *Rhetoric, Poetics,* and *Nicomachean Powerpointia.*

YOUR AUDIENCE

Who is your audience? This, of course, is an empirical question. Our vast, comprehensive examination of the extant demography literature has revealed the following dimensions of typical academic audiences:

- *Garrulity Intolerance:* Your audience wants you to avoid going over the allotted time; they are happy if your talk ends a bit early.
- *Relative Intelligence Differential:* As you feared, many people in the audience are smarter than you.
- *Angle of Repose (aka Stegner Factor):* Your audience happens to be sitting down, whereas you are standing up.
- *Geographic-Temporal Conjunction:* Your audience prefers to sit in the back because psychologists tend to be tardy.

In short, your audience bears an eerie resemblance to you when you're listening instead of speaking. You are vaguely curious about the talk and willing to enter into the tacit contract with the speaker: "I'll sit quietly, listen politely, and keep my snarky questions to myself, provided that you don't insult my intelligence or talk too long. My time is short, my caffeine addiction is strong, and my bladder is small." Woe unto the speaker who violates this contract.

Beyond these generalities, different kinds of talks attract different crowds. We'll describe these audiences in more detail in later chapters; for now, here are a few examples:

- For conference talks and posters, your audience will resemble the general conference crowd. Local and regional conferences attract a lot of undergraduates; national and international meetings have proportionally more professors and sometimes clinical professionals. In general, the audience knows a lot about the area of research.

- For job talks, your audience will include a lot of professors, many graduate and undergraduate students (depending on the institution), and possibly a few administrators.
- For talks to lay audiences, you'll have curious, intelligent adults who chose to spend their time listening to you despite their reasonable fear that you'll ramble in jargon.

WHY PEOPLE SHOW UP, PART 1

Teaching (or attending) undergraduate lectures distorts your tacit knowledge of how to relate to an audience. Undergrads are trapped, and they remind you of it with their exasperated sighs, raucous backpack zippers, and expressions of sullen detachment. Teaching is good practice in some ways—it helps people get over public-speaking anxiety, for example—but bad practice in other ways. A trapped audience will stay seated and takes notes because of the carrot of extra credit and the eucalyptus branch of exams.

Unlike students, scholarly audiences are there because they want to be. A conference audience can always leave to check out the posters, browse the exhibit booths, attend another talk, or ditch the conference in favor of the nearby aquarium. You must respect your audience's time—people aren't obligated to listen to you, and you aren't entitled to an audience. You are not touring the prison system, playing Joan Baez songs on your acoustic guitar to an audience with nothing better to do than lift weights and tattoo each other. Your audience probably has something else to do after your talk. If necessary, they'll get up and walk out.

Speaking too long is a cardinal sin of public speaking. Never do this. We don't mean "try to avoid going over your time" or "it would be bad if you talked too long"—we mean don't do this even once. You shouldn't break the tacit speaker–audience contract, cut into another speaker's time, or present yourself as a beginner. You can do two things to prevent talking too long. First, time yourself during your rehearsal talks. If the talk is too long, trim it. Second, imagine a burly koala sitting in the front row, squinting his eyes and shifting a vaudeville hook from paw to paw.

As a rule of paw, use only 80% of your time, at most. For a 15-minute conference talk, this gives you 12 minutes to talk and 3 minutes to answer questions. For an hour-long talk, this gives you 48 minutes to talk and 12 minutes to answer questions. If you expect a lot of questions—for example, if you're giving a job talk or a workshop—then use even less time. When Paul gives hour-long talks to graduate students about academic writing, he aims for 40 minutes; when Dave gives hour-and-a-half-long talks about end-of-life care to lay audiences, he tries not to talk for more than 45 minutes. Controlling your time will earn you the goodwill and respect of your audience. No one ever thought, "That talk wasn't long enough. I was hoping for another 10 minutes of implications for future research."

WHY PEOPLE SHOW UP, PART 2

Undergrad teaching often involves "covering material": explaining classic studies, reinforcing fundamentals, and preparing students for advanced classes that build on the one you're teaching. Because you have your students for a semester, you've got time to cover most of what strikes your fancy. But you have your conference audience for only a few minutes, and you aren't testing them afterward. This is why it's important to be selective and focused.

It's easier to focus your talk when you realize that the audience is sophisticated. At a typical conference, for example, there may be six sessions of talks at time, each on a different topic. People showed up to your session because they are knowledgeable, curious, or willing to learn; you also can presume that they know a good deal about the broad area of research. This is true for conference presentations aimed at undergrads, too. The slackers didn't bother to attend the conference, so you have a motivated audience.

Focus on what's new about your topic. For research talks, cover what you did and what you found. You needn't review the basic concepts and history in much detail, if at all. It's better to give your audience too much credit than too little. The beginners in the audience know that they're beginners—they won't be mad that you gave them too much credit. But the experts may resent being patronized. We saw an example of this recently at a regional conference. A well-known researcher was giving an hour-long talk about new research on clinical disorders across the life span. He spent almost half the talk reviewing the *DSM* criteria for a dozen disorders. Apart from being boring, this was insulting to the sophisticated crowd. Several people walked out. A brief recap of the disorders would have sufficed.

For practical talks, your audience wants to learn something useful, such as how to be a better writer, teacher, mentor, or counselor. Focus on what your audience could do after they leave the conference, not what they should think or feel. We're not saying you should never discuss thoughts and feelings, but advice founded on behavior will be more practical. For example, imagine that you attended a conference session on how to finish your dissertation and submit it to a journal. The speaker could say, "Take heart—it will be over one day," or "Think about what your dissertation really means to you." This advice might sound inspiring during the talk, but it's mushy and insubstantial. As an audience member, you want concrete behavioral advice that will help, such as, "Pick 6 hours a week to write, and write during those hours" and "Go to the journal's webpage, read the submission guidelines, and follow them exactly."

FINDING OUT WHO IS IN YOUR AUDIENCE

If you've attended a conference before, you probably have a good idea about what your audience will be like. Standard talks will catch a cross-section of the conference audience. A session called "How to Survive Your Dissertation" will attract frazzled grad students; a group of talks called "Understanding Rural Substance Abuse" will attract people interested in substance abuse and a few farmers looking to score some meth.

Paul's Woeful Tale of Woe

Talks are crafted for audiences, so disasters can ensue when the audience is changed at the last minute. It's rare that an audience is switched on you, but it has happened to me a few times. At one of my job interviews, a professor on the search committee told me, "Oh, I invited my undergrad social psychology class to your talk. Do you think you could change it a bit to engage them?" Being young and overconfident, I said, "Sure." That was foolish of me. My talk was about the joint operation of cognitive-consistency systems. It had all the glorious technical details that professors love, but it must have been abominably boring for the undergraduates who made up 80% of the audience. My improvised attempts to connect to them were forced and pitiful. I'm sure my talk convinced at least a third of the students to change their major.

With time, you can anticipate your audience. For example, I often give talks about academic writing to graduate students. When I ask who will show up, I often hear, "Oh, around 100 graduate students from different departments. You might get one or two faculty, too." For my first talk, I crafted the presentation for graduate students involving some prickly jokes at the expense of professors. Unfortunately, professors turned out to be 20% of the audience, and those jokes didn't work in mixed company. After giving a few of these talks, I've learned to expect a diverse crowd: assistant professors, composition instructors, crafty undergrads, people

(continued)

who work in the campus writing center, people avoiding the rain, and students in public-speaking courses attending as a class assignment. By far, the professors are the most comical: Sometimes they slink in and sit in the back, abashed at crashing an event advertised for graduate students.

Things get trickier if you aren't speaking to a standard conference audience, such as when you give invited talks, colloquia, or workshops. If you're not sure who will be attending your talk, feel free to interrogate whoever invited you to speak. For example, here are some good things to ask if you are invited to give a practical talk to an audience of graduate students.

- How many people will show up?
- How many will be graduate students?
- What areas of research are they studying?
- How far along in grad school are they?
- Do they have any training in this already?
- For what sick reasons are they attending a workshop on zero-inflated negative binomial models?
- Were they dropped as children?

SPEAKING TO INTERNATIONAL AUDIENCES

English has emerged as a global language of science. Nearly all international conferences are conducted in English—a convenient arrangement for us, but a bad deal for the vast non-English-speaking world. All of your audiences will have at least a few nonnative speakers; at national and international meetings, nonnative speakers might make up most of the audience. You can show respect for your multilingual listeners by slowing down, avoiding slang, and evaluating whether your jokes will make sense. Although they obviously speak English, they won't understand you if you talk like a Merry Prankster from *The Electric Kool-Aid Acid Test*. You needn't use the deliberate enunciation that preschool teachers use, but you could at least drop the *Dawson's Creek* jokes.

You probably got the *Dawson's Creek* reference but missed the *Acid Test* reference. (Don't worry—it wasn't funny.) Think of your foreign audience as a large group of people who never read *The Electric Kool-Aid Acid Test*, and you'll be okay.

If English isn't your native language, then you speak to foreigners all the time. Many nonnative speakers have told us that they feel nervous when talking to a group of English speakers; the anxiety of speaking is aggravated by the difficulty of speaking in a foreign language. Rest assured, however, that your audience won't be silently judging your English, wincing at every error. On the contrary, they'll admire you for giving an academic talk in English. To explain why, we must confront the seamy reality of American academics.

Relative to Americans in general, American psychologists lean left: We tend to know too much about books and too little about tattoos. If you need conversation starters at the next conference, just ask, "What's the local NPR station?" or "Is there a farmer's market near the conference hotel?" Being the leftist agitators that we are, we support mandatory foreign-language instruction in elementary schools; being Americans, we don't speak a foreign language ourselves. When we see a foreigner giving a professional talk, we are filled with leftist agitator shame. There is something to be said for making a few mistakes, thus calling attention to your linguistic dominance. If you speak English too well, you won't get credit for giving a talk in a foreign language; your audience might think that you moved to Europe after growing up in Denver.

In short, don't worry: You have an understanding audience. The lone exception, of course, is when Canadian speakers say "zed" for the letter Z. We Americans find that hilarious.

PONDEROUS REFLECTIONS AND CONCLUSIONS

Knowing your audience allows you to craft a good talk. Your audience has no obligation to be there, so keep your talk short; your audience knows a lot about your topic, so keep your talk relevant and focused. If you take your listeners' perspective when planning your talk, you can avoid most public-speaking disasters and most hook-wielding koalas—but Aristotle could have told you that.

3

Preparing and Delivering Your Talk

There are many tasks involved in proposing, planning, and delivering a talk. Depending on the type of talk, you may have to choose a venue; submit an abstract; write the talk; create PowerPoint slides; and of course, deliver the cursed thing. If you're the kind of person who is always organized, these tasks may seem painfully simple. If you're organizationally challenged, however, the process may seem simply painful. In this chapter, we'll offer concrete tips for everything from writing the presentation and developing effective PowerPoint slides to practicing and delivering your talk. But first, we should address what, for many people, is the most challenging aspect of developing a talk—the battle with procrastination.

VANQUISHING PROCRASTINATION

Anxiety and fear are powerful impediments to public speaking. If you were about to jump out of an airplane, every fiber of your being would likely cry out, "Don't do it!" You may experience this same phenomenon when planning a presentation—we call it *procrastination*, the evil demon that stalks you from the shadows and tells you to watch reruns of *The Benny Hill Show*. This demon's nefarious ways are bolstered by a number of false beliefs about public speaking. Although experienced speakers know that these beliefs are 100% grade-A berserk, they can be powerfully convincing to newbies.

"Talks Are Better When They're Spontaneous, So I Shouldn't Prepare Much"

Some people believe that insufficient planning somehow will make their presentation more exciting. Although less planning will certainly lead to a more spontaneous talk, it's likely to be awful. You'll look disorganized and sloppy. If you're a more experienced speaker, it's okay to allow some breathing room in your talk for spontaneity. For instance, after giving gazillions of talks on similar topics, the same jokes may get tired. If you're quick-witted enough, it's not a bad idea to allow flexibility for new quips. Beginners, however, shouldn't even think about it.

"Preparing My Talk Early Will Just Make Me Nervous, So I Should Put It Off"

This is a common one. We've even seen this offered as "good" advice in other books and on websites on public speaking. In our opinion, this is nonsense. Practice and planning make things easier. Research on social facilitation (Zajonc, 1965) shows that people perform relatively complex, highly practiced tasks better in the presence of others than when others aren't present. On the other hand, people perform unpracticed tasks worse when others are present than when they're not. In other words, practice is your best bet for performing well in front of an audience.

"It's Just A Short Talk, So I Don't Really Need To Prepare"

This is a favorite belief of nervous procrastinators everywhere. In case you doubt us, take a look at Dave's Woeful Tale of Woe. This belief both minimizes the difficulty of the task and lets you off the hook for preparation. The reason it's so convincing is that it's true, sort of. You're probably going to spend less time preparing for a 15-minute research presentation than for an hour-long keynote address. Nonetheless, you still have to plan. The key is to spend enough time preparing given the type of presentation you'll be giving.

Dave's Woeful Tale of Woe

I abhor airplane flights. If you're a psychologist, you know why: As soon as the people seated next to you discover what you do, they either become horribly frightened and ignore you or they tell you all about their 30-year-old son in Idaho who tricks out cars and refuses to get a job. The exception to this rule involves flights to conferences. For some reason, I always wind up sitting next to other psychologists. You can tell who they are: They're the ones

---

(continued)

with their laptops out, furiously working on PowerPoint slides. They're also the ones assiduously avoiding eye contact lest they hear about someone's car-detailing offspring.

A few years ago, I broke the silence. I was curious why the nicely dressed, obviously seasoned psychologist seated next to me was still working on his presentation only one day before the conference. He smiled and said, "It's really no big deal. I give these things all the time." Because the topic was intriguing, I decided to attend his talk the next day. The research was as interesting as I expected, but the presentation style was horrible. He didn't seem to know what slide was coming up next, often needed to backtrack and start sentences over, and went over on time.

I've certainly been there: Despite my better judgment, I put off writing the presentation until it's almost too late. Working furiously on the airplane or in my hotel room, I reassure myself that "I'm an expert at giving talks" and "it's no big deal." Sorry, even seasoned speakers need preparation and practice, and it is a big deal. The people in the audience are friendly, but they expect you to take their time seriously. You'd want the same, right?

The best way to combat procrastination is to intentionally schedule time to work on your talk. Preparing a talk, like writing an article, requires some motivational tools (Silvia, 2007).

■ Make a schedule. When you're working on a complex task, it's not enough to have faith that it will get done, especially if you tend to procrastinate. "I'll do it tomorrow" is an easy way to reduce anxiety in the short-term, but it's bound to increase it later. Instead, schedule a couple hours a week to do nothing but work on your talk. Knowing that you only have to work on the talk for this brief period will reduce your anxiety and help you complete the necessary tasks more efficiently.

- Set goals. There are many steps in the process of submitting, planning, practicing, and delivering a talk. Some of these steps, like submitting an abstract, are time sensitive. For this reason, it's a good idea to take out a calendar and write approximate dates by which you'd like finish each task. Of course, which and how many particular tasks you list will depend on the type of talk and how anal-retentive you are.

- Monitor progress. Research shows that concrete positive feedback regarding progress toward a goal increases motivation (Snyder, 1994). When you're in the middle of planning a talk, it's easy to miss how much headway you're making. That's why it's important to monitor your progress. A simple way to monitor progress involves listing all the tasks necessary to prepare the presentation. When you accomplish one, simply check it off. Make sure the list is long and detailed enough that you get to check something off every week.

- Make public commitments. Letting others know about your self-imposed deadlines is a great way to keep yourself motivated. Tell your friend John that you plan to submit that abstract by August 11. Let your sister Sally know that you're shooting to have the PowerPoint slides ready by November 4. Finally, ask your colleague Vyacheslavovich to listen to you deliver a draft of the talk on November 12. You wouldn't want to disappoint them, would you?

WRITING YOUR TALK

Now that you've set your schedule, laid out some goals, and committed yourself to work on your talk, it's time to get started writing. How you go about writing your talk will undoubtedly depend on the type of presentation it is. A research presentation will differ hugely from a poster or a talk for the lay public. We'll discuss each of these presentation formats in detail later in the book. For now, let's cover some general tips for writing your talk.

Develop a Clear Statement of Your Objectives

Before writing, spend some time thinking about your objectives. Two broad categories of objectives are useful to consider: informational and attitudinal. *Informational* objectives consist of the type and amount of information you want your listeners to gain. An informational objective of this chapter, for instance, is for you to learn the steps in preparing a talk. *Attitudinal* objectives, on the other hand, consist of how you would like your audience to change their beliefs as a result of the talk. Two attitudinal objectives for this chapter are for you to learn to value the importance of preparation and to fear the coming koala apocalypse. Both types of objectives should serve as guidelines as you write your talk.

We recommend sharing informational objectives with the audience. At the beginning of your talk, you might say something like, "My goals in this talk are to detail the koalas' strategy for worldwide domination as well as to discuss what we know about how Bernese mountain dogs are leading an underground resistance." This gives the audience a sense of what they should be listening for during the presentation. Attitudinal objectives, however, are best kept to yourself. Audiences can get defensive if they think you're trying to manipulate them (which, of course, you are).

Plan an Opening Strategy

An "opening strategy" is the first thing that comes out of your mouth when you begin your talk. Effective opening strategies put the audience at ease and grab their attention. A brief joke or humorous cartoon can serve as a great opening strategy. In a presentation for clinicians on helping patients choose an appropriate setting for end-of-life care, for instance, Dave displayed a cartoon of the grim reaper talking to a woman in a bar; the caption read, "Your place or mine?" If you can't think of a joke relevant to your topic, consider sharing an intriguing anecdote or provocative statistic. If nothing comes to mind, simply thank your audience for their attention and convey your pleasure in being with them.

**Include Brief Introductory
and Conclusion Statements**

Remember when you first learned to write an essay? Undoubtedly, the teacher told you to begin by saying what you're going to say, then say it, and finally summarize what you said. Presentations are no different. We recommend following your opening strategy with a brief statement of what you'll be talking about. A good way to do this is simply to share your informational objectives. You can review these objectives again at the end of the presentation as a way of summarizing and concluding. If you want to be really snazzy, you also could leave your audience with a take-away message. A take-away message of this chapter might be, "There are lots of steps involved in giving a talk, but with proper preparation, anybody can do it."

Tell a Story

Stories are one of your most effective tools in public speaking. Yes, we realize they're not scientific or generalizable. We've even heard some faculty mentors advise students against the use of stories. Nonetheless, people like them. Although anecdotes should never take the place of hard data, they can wonderfully illustrate those data. They put a human face on the abstractions of our field. For these reasons, if you've got extra time in your presentation, we highly recommend telling a brief story to demonstrate how the concepts and data you're presenting appear in the real world.

Don't Write Every Word of Your Presentation

This is one of the most common mistakes among novice presenters. If you're nervous about giving a talk, you might find yourself thinking, "If I write it out word for word, all I'll have to do is read it." Although technically true, this is unbelievably boring. And what happens if you look up from your notes and lose your place? Suddenly you'll be fumbling around trying to regain your bearings. In contrast, we recommend choosing one of two strategies. First, you can scrap the notes altogether and use PowerPoint slides to cue you. This is the best strategy because you won't have to constantly shift your attention from notes to the projector screen. If you must have notes, however, we recommend creating only a brief outline of your talk. Don't use complete sentences or long statements; simply write down a few words to cue you about what to say. The key to preparing good notes is that you should never be tempted to read from them.

Use PowerPoint Wisely

Now that we've advised you to use PowerPoint instead of notes, we should add a few words of warning. People too often use PowerPoint as a crutch. They may write every word of their talk on the slides and then just read them. This is incredibly annoying, so don't do it. Because this infuriating practice is so pervasive, the subsequent section is dedicated to the proper use of PowerPoint.

DEVELOPING POWERPOINT SLIDES

PowerPoint is a controversial subject for experienced presenters. Some love it, others hate it. Dave, for instance, refuses to use PowerPoint when he teaches courses at

31

his university. Nonetheless, PowerPoint is a fact of life for conferences and job talks. Not using it in these contexts will make you look like a Luddite.

Perhaps you've heard the rumors that PowerPoint presentations reduce learning in comparison with old-school techniques. Dave has been fond of quoting this supposed research finding to his colleagues. Unfortunately, after having searched the literature, he's embarrassed to admit that the picture isn't so clear. Researchers have found that PowerPoint can either increase or decrease the amount your audience learns, depending on how you use it.

Let's start with the bad stuff first. Presenting the same material both orally and visually is a very bad idea. According to cognitive load theory (Sweller & Chandler, 1991), it takes serious cognitive resources to interpret verbal material. Much like RAM memory in a computer, people have only so many cognitive resources to go around. So, if you're listening to speech, you're using some of your cognitive resources to make sense of the message being conveyed. Likewise, if you're reading PowerPoint slides, you're using resources to interpret the text. Here's the problem: If you're *both* reading and listening to the same material, you're using double the cognitive resources necessary. This leaves fewer resources to understand the material and commit it to memory. Perhaps this is why research demonstrates that when speech and PowerPoint slides are redundant, the audience both feels more mentally taxed and learns significantly less than when the material is presented only orally (Kalyuga, Chandler, & Sweller, 2004; Leahy, Sweller, & Chandler, 2003). In case we haven't said it enough, don't just read your PowerPoint slides.

But PowerPoint isn't all bad. When oral and visual materials aren't redundant, the audience learns more from presentations using PowerPoint than when information is presented only orally (Leahy et al., 2003). Moreover, multimedia features like video clips can have positive effects on learning (Hallett & Faria, 2006). When used properly, PowerPoint presentations appear to increase listeners' self-efficacy and enjoyment of the material being presented (Susskind, 2008).

With these facts in mind, here are a few tips for using PowerPoint.

Use PowerPoint to Prompt You, Not Replace You

The key to good PowerPoint presentations is using the slides to supplement rather than supplant your oral presentation. Think of your PowerPoint slides as a schematic or outline of your presentation rather than a word-for-word transcript. To keep you honest, we recommend limiting yourself to about 40 words per slide divided among no more than four bullet points. If you do the math, this means your font size will be about 30 points—perfect for easy viewing. Uncrowded slides mean your audience will waste less energy paying attention to the projector and will learn more from your presentation. Check out the examples in Figure 3.1.

FIGURE 3.1. Examples of bad and good PowerPoint slides. The top slide is cluttered and difficult to read. The bottom slide is much simpler and is easy to read.

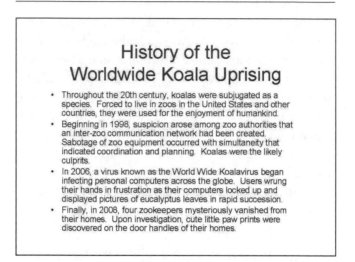

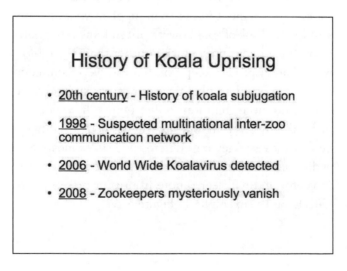

Use Diagrams to Illustrate Your Points

One of PowerPoint's most useful features is its ability to display graphics and video. Research shows that the use of these bells and whistles increases learning (Hallett & Faria, 2006). Bar and line graphs, for instance, are much more effective ways of presenting data than tables full of means, parameters, and asterisks. Flow charts and other diagrams are great ways of presenting theories and experimental methods. Last, photographs and cartoons can add comical and human elements to your presentation. For examples of good and bad ways to present information, see Figure 3.2.

Keep It Simple

Believe it or not, there's a whole area of research investigating the effects of typeface and slide background on recall of information. No kidding. Some experts say that information presented using *sans serif* fonts—the plainer typefaces such as Arial, Verdana, and Helvetica—leads to the greatest learning (Wilder & Rotondo, 2002). In contrast, some claim that *serif* fonts like Times New Roman do the best job, mainly because their fabulous little curlicues lend elegance to the presentation (Endicott, 1999). Other researchers find that certain sans serif as well as some serif fonts are good, whereas others aren't (Kingery & Furuta, 1997). Still other researchers—probably most—don't care. Given these inconclusive findings, don't spend too much time obsessing over fonts; just choose a

FIGURE 3.2. Ineffective and effective ways of visually presenting information. The top slide shows an ineffective way of displaying data. The bottom slide shows an effective use of graphics to display data.

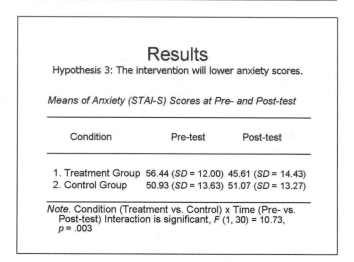

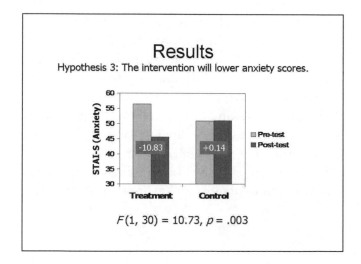

standard font that most computers will have. For what it's worth, graphic designers strongly prefer sans serif fonts for presentations (see Reynolds, 2008).

Slide background, however, may be more important. Some evidence indicates that complex backgrounds distract audiences, reducing recall of information (Larson, 2004). Yes, we like the fancy background with the goldfish pond, too. That doesn't mean you have to use it.

Keep It Short

We've all seen presentations where the speaker runs out of time and winds up skipping through the last 20 PowerPoint slides at a breakneck pace. It doesn't take a rocket scientist to realize that you can't cover 60 slides in 15 minutes unless you're that guy who talks really fast at the end of drug company commercials. As a rule of thumb, we recommend no more than one slide per minute. It's not a contest to see how many slides you can get through. Instead, use the tips just covered to create simple and efficiently structured slides that convey sufficient information in limited space.

PRACTICING YOUR TALK

After planning your talk, it's time to practice. How you do this will depend on your level of confidence and experience. For beginners, we advise a two-step approach. First, practice your talk by yourself. This can be done in a comfortable, low-pressure way. For instance, Dave and Paul do this sitting at their desks at home. Speak out loud at the pace you plan to use during the presentation. Although you may look a little crazy talking to your computer, it's a great way of making sure you're happy with the content, organization, and timing of the talk. When you're finished, make any necessary corrections and run through the talk again.

When you're satisfied with the results from Step 1, the next step is to practice in front of others. This is especially helpful if this is your first talk or if you want feedback. This doesn't have to be complicated. Just ask a friend or two to sit through your talk. If you're a graduate student and belong to a lab group, ask your professor if it would be possible to use some meeting time to practice. Give your presentation in a formal way, just as you would during the conference.

Afterward, ask for constructive feedback. Hopefully, you'll get both positive and negative comments. Whatever the audience tells you, consider adjusting your presentation to take it into account. But don't get discouraged. Remember that you've asked for feedback; getting it doesn't mean you've done badly.

Delivering your Talk

You've carefully prepared and practiced your talk, you've created a handful of killer PowerPoint slides that illustrate your main points, you've even done a few dry runs. Now it's the big moment. Here are a few tips to improve your performance.

As we already belabored in Chapter 2, too many speakers use more than their allotted time. If you've carefully planned and practiced your talk, this is unlikely to occur. Nerves can make strange things happen, however. Sometimes people wind up talking much slower or faster than usual. The easiest way to avoid this is to bring along a small timer or stop watch. Make sure it's big enough that you can see it from your standing position so you're not tempted to constantly pick it up and look at it. Such behavioral tics can annoy audiences and distract them from what you're saying.

Remember that girl in high school who got up in front of the class to deliver her presentation on "The State of Florida: Not Just Old People Anymore," and began a convulsive giggling fit? You probably won't have that problem, but you may inadvertently engage in any number of other nervous tics. Maybe you bite your lip, wring your hands, or play with your hair. Before PowerPoint was en vogue, Dave once saw a presentation where the speaker compulsively adjusted the overhead transparency. He couldn't get the text totally straight on the screen, so he just kept trying. It was like watching a little earthquake. One could feel the audience restrain itself from a collective slapping fit.

We all do this stuff. Dave paces; Paul eats bugs. Controlling yourself for a few minutes will help you to connect with your audience. If you have trouble remembering not to indulge in your tic, try Dave's method: He sticks a note that says "Don't pace!" to the corner of his laptop's screen.

An equally common mistake among beginning presenters involves saying something like, "Sorry, everybody, I'm really nervous." People do this to get the audience on their side. The logic goes like this: "I'm nervous, so if I share this with the audience, they won't think I'm stupid if I mess up." The problem with this strategy is that it doesn't work. It just makes everyone else nervous, too. In our experience, the audience is already on your side. They know you're nervous and want you to succeed. In fact, a lot of them are thinking, "I'm glad I'm not up there right now." Instead of highlighting your nervousness, stay cool, stare danger straight in the eyes, and begin with your opening strategy.

While you're looking danger in the eyes, be sure to do the same for your audience. We know that you already know this. Nonetheless, you'd be surprised how many people don't follow this rule. At one conference, Dave watched a speaker deliver his entire presentation facing away from the audience. This exemplified two cardinal errors. First, the speaker was just reading from PowerPoint slides. And second, he never once looked at the audience. Although the content of the talk was interesting, it was difficult to stay engaged without occasional eye contact from the speaker. Besides, it was just weird.

Although following these tips will make your presentation go as smoothly as possible, unforeseen problems can still occur. The good news is that they're generally small. Perhaps the microphone stops working, you forget to pass out your handouts, you fumble your words, or there is a sudden koala attack. Dave once gave a job talk in which his PowerPoint remote kept advancing slides by itself; Paul has had enough projector crashes to create persecutory delusions. You can't prevent all possible problems. The key is to be nice to yourself. If you mess up, just correct the error and move on. If a quick joke comes to mind, feel free to share it. But don't beat yourself up; the audience isn't. Why make yourself into the meanest person in the room? For more on unforeseen disasters, take a look at Chapter 6.

PONDEROUS REFLECTIONS AND CONCLUSIONS

The advice in this chapter has been relatively general in scope, covering tips that should work regardless of the type of talk you're preparing. We'll offer tips tailored to specific presentation formats in the second half of the book. But we've said enough for now. Go write the thing already.

4

Answering Questions

Being a college professor is a fun job. We're glad we chose academics instead of opera (Dave's backup) or homelessness (Paul's backup). But like all jobs, it has its grim moments. Teaching public speaking to students is like teaching obedience classes for rescued pit bulls: Your first goal is to prevent people from getting mauled—teaching the fancy tricks comes later. These classes are painful for the students and awkward for us. But it's our job: We take a deep breath, dab ourselves with koala repellent, and plunge into the maelstrom.

Our students say they fear the questions more than the talk. Most beginners fear thinking on their feet: What if I get stumped? What if I freeze? What if someone picks on me? But we've found that most people are better public answerers than public speakers. During their talks, our students look awkward, their voices stammer, their feet shuffle, their eyes float above the audience. But during the questions, the students stand still, gesture normally, and speak conversationally. The speaker looks stilted and formal; the answerer looks interested and engaged, like someone who cares enough about the topic to study it.

Good speakers are typically good answerers, but it's possible to do only one part well. Some people are ebullient speakers but defensive, surly answerers: They brook no dissent or criticism. Other people are abominable speakers, reading aloud from a paper, but are witty and insightful when forced to abandon their script. Answering questions is an art: It has its own rules, norms, and decorum. This chapter teaches you the craft of this art.

QUESTIONS ARE IMPORTANT

We think that the questions are the most revealing part of the presentation. It isn't hard, with some practice, to give a good canned talk. You needn't know what you're talking about—an actor, for example, could memorize 12 minutes of material and unleash a dynamic presentation about lexical priming of cross-language cognates in a bilingual sample. (One often wishes, in fact, that researchers would subcontract their talks to trained actors.) Because questions are unpredictable, your responses illuminate your academic sophistication, personality, and poise.

For some kinds of presentations, the questions overshadow the talk. Job talks, for example, are closer to public interrogation—collegial interrogation, naturally—

than to public speaking. Presenting a poster is mostly a matter of answering questions and thinking on your feet. For these genres, the prepared remarks are a way of starting a conversation: The questions are the heart of the thing.

One simple reason why questions are important is that they happen at the end. According to the peak–end rule (e.g., Fredrickson, 2000), people's judgments of an event are largely affected by its peak (the quality of its best part) and end (the quality of its last part). If your talk ends well, people will remember it well, even if most of it was mediocre. If it ends awkwardly—such as with you blanking on easy questions, fidgeting defensively with your laser pointer, and giving curt answers—your audience will think that you're weird and mean. (If it ends with a wallaby dropping from the rafters and snarling in the ineffectual manner peculiar to wallabies, no one will remember your talk. Hence, always stash an "emergency wallaby" in the rafters.)

UNDERSTANDING THE NORMS

Conferences, like all social gatherings, have social norms. You see norms in action when you experience a sense of *should* and *ought:* How formally should I dress? Is it tacky to hand out business cards? Should I pack my tattoo equipment? If you've attended a few conferences, you already know the norms for questions. For brief talks, the audience will generally wait until the end to ask questions—you needn't remind them to hold their inquisitive water. For longer talks, you can choose to invite questions during the talk. If you don't say anything, people will generally wait until the end. Paul prefers to invite people to ask questions if the urge strikes; Dave invites midtalk questions for his long talks but not for shorter ones.

Many audience members will save their questions for after the session, so stick around to see if anyone wants to talk with you. Some scientists are shy and socially awkward—unimaginable, we know—so they would rather ask you one on one than in a large group. Some questions are too complex to handle in the brief time available during the session. And some questions would seem strange to ask in a question-and-answer period, like "Hey, could you e-mail me some of your papers about this topic?"

Conferences have firm norms for politeness. You will rarely face a hostile crowd. Your audience might gossip about you behind your back, but they won't maul you during your talk. In this respect, the conference world is nicer than our daily world. Graduate students, for example, face some tough crowds. During defense meetings, the professors might grill you merely to see how you handle questions under pressure. In grad seminars, students will interrogate each other simply to show off, to poke fun, or to continue their interminable battle over the office thermostat. Graduate school is meant to toughen people up for the cold, cruel world, which turns out to be uncold and uncruel.

The politeness norms apply to you, too. As the speaker, you should respect the people who took the time to listen to your talk. Imagine, for example, seeing these presentation titles in the conference program:

- Art Therapy as Pseudoscience
- New Research on the Biology of Race and Gender Differences in Intelligence
- What's Wrong With Cognitive Psychology?
- The Myth of Giftedness: How to Dismantle Gifted Education
- All of You Are Wrong and I Am Right: Further Support for the "I'm Always Right" (IAR) Model

Those talks would have fun question-and-answer periods. If you want to provoke your audience, it isn't hard: Pick on other researchers; dismiss large bodies of work; or make sweeping, unsupported claims. There are scholarly ways to discuss disagreements; save your nonscholarly scuffles for the airport shuttle.

Playing nice with others extends to how you answer questions. If you respond rudely, pretentiously, or haughtily to the first question, you might not get a second one. We've seen a few creepy talks in which a charismatic speaker became snippy when answering questions. "Ah," the audience thinks. "That guy is nice-veneer-over-a-putrid-core-of-narcissism charming, not nice-person charming." If you're a narcissist, there's no point to telling you not to act like a stuck-up jerk. But if you're merely nervous, we suggest that you don't act like a stuck-up jerk.

Inviting and Answering Questions

You should start the question period by inviting questions. It's easy to do, but many talks end gracelessly. Some presenters keep clicking through their slides, run into the black final slide, and say, "Oh, okay, I guess that's it." They seem surprised, like they expected seven more slides. Other presenters don't say even that—they stare blankly at the audience, fidgeting with the laser pointer and waiting for the deluge. We've seen a few people begin the question period defensively by saying, "Okay, let me have it," or "Well, do your worst." Even the wallabies lurking in the rafters wince when they hear that. Who wants to ask a question in response to "Let me have it"? Such statements convey "I'm nervous and I think you're hostile. Don't ask anything." To help you begin the question period on a right foot, here are a few tips.

- Start simple. Just say something like, "Thanks. Can I answer any questions?" That's it. If you must be different, you can try bold, experimental variants, such as "Thanks for listening. Does anyone have any questions?" or "Thank you. Are there any questions?" If you like, you can insert a final slide that invites questions. It's nicer to have a slide up during questions than to have the bleak black screen. Figure 4.1 shows two slides that Paul has used. (The pairing of the vintage George Nelson chair and upside-down turtle has some dark, psychoanalytic meaning—don't ask.)

FIGURE 4.1. Examples of wrap-up slides that invite questions.

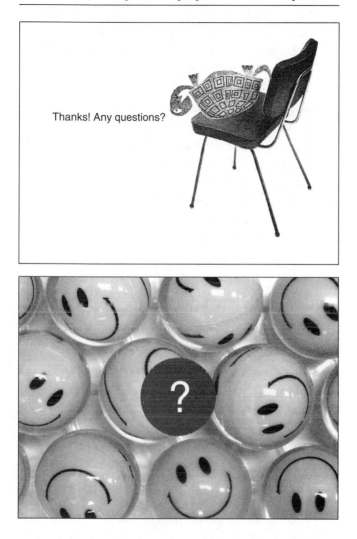

- Use nondefensive body language. Your body language will betray you if you're feeling defensive. Many presenters lean away from the audience, step back a few feet, or fold their arms over their chest. This looks bad. Defensive gestures discourage questions and make you look weird. If you do nothing else, just stand still and listen to the questions. We recommend, though, that you use the "walk toward the question" technique. In this complex, demanding, and multistep maneuver, you walk toward the person asking the question. You'll hear the question better, and your body language will be positive instead of avoidant.

- Keep your time in mind. We suspect that this advice is fruitless: The desire to give a subtle, reflective answer to even the simplest question beats strong in the hearts of psychologists. But for short talks, you'll need to keep a lid on it—there isn't enough time for the standard exegesis. Consider the typical 15-minute conference talk. If you apply the 20% rule (see Chapter 2), you have only 3 minutes for questions. That's time for only 2 or 3 questions, depending on the long-windedness of the parties involved. For long talks, though, feel free to unleash.

- What if you get no questions? This happens a lot at conferences; it usually isn't personal, but it could be. Blunt silence is often your audience's way of telling you that you took too long. If you went over your time, the audience will respect the next speaker's allotted time. If the session is nearly over, the audience's desire to go to the bathroom and get coffee competes with the desire to interrogate you about your research. Don't worry about it. Just say "Thanks" and sit down.

ANTICIPATING QUESTIONS

With some experience, you can anticipate the questions that people will ask you. For whatever reason, audiences usually will ask you the same questions every time you give a talk. With some allowance for grievance and confusion, here are the major classes of questions, written as question stems, that you'll get for a research talk. If you have attended a few conferences, these will sound familiar. You can fill in the brackets with your research topic.

Detail, Circumscription, and Generality

People usually ask about the boundaries of your work: the details, the limitations, and the possible generalizations.

- "Do you think you would find the same thing if you [studied both men and women, collected data in a collectivistic culture, didn't use the subject pool, omitted feral children from the sample]?"
- "How exactly did you measure [risk for depression, hope, eucalyptus allergies]?"
- "Do you think you found what you found because you had a sample of [college students, at-risk-youth, falconers]?"

Theory to Practice to Theory

Applied researchers will want to hear about practical uses of your research; basic researchers will want to hear about the implications for technical theories. Theory-to-practice questions are probably more common than practice-to-theory questions.

- "Do you think this research could help [cognitive–behavioral treatments for depression, early interventions for adolescent addiction, animal wrangling]?"
- "Does this work have any implications for [theories of depression, models of impulsivity, object-relations theory]?"

Past and Present

Some audience members may ask how your current work will inform future research; other questions ask how your current work is informed by past research. In job talks, you'll always get the "what comes next?" question.

- "Where will you go next with your work on [goals and well-being, personality and mental health, urban forestry]?"
- "There's a long history of interest in this topic. How do you see your work in relation to [Fritz Heider's naive psychology, early behavior therapies for anxiety, the span of modern Western thought]?"

HANDLING THE AGGRIEVED AND THE CONFUSED

Beginners fear getting grilled by a mean audience member. If you fear hostile questions, take a moment to visualize your imagined antagonist. Perhaps the swirl of imagination yields an image of a scowling, overweight man with grey hair, a frayed jacket, and a notepad full of aggressive questions. (Granted, there are many overweight men with ill-fitting jackets at conferences, but they're generally amiable.) Perhaps your imagined antagonist has an eerie resemblance to your grad school advisor. Perhaps he is short and hairy, gnawing grumpily on a eucalyptus branch.

In our careers, we have had many socially graceless questioners—people with overly persistent, confusing, or eccentric questions—but only one mean questioner (see Dave's Woeful Tale of Woe in Chapter 9). It has rarely happened, and we have talked to some tough crowds. Unless you're speaking about a touchy topic, you'll drive your audience to mild interest or to mild sleepiness, not to narrow-eyed anger. For better or worse, your audience doesn't know you well enough to dislike you.

Mean questioners are out there, living their thwarted, embittered lives, grumbling about their grievances to their dogs, but we doubt that you'll run into them during your first few talks. And if you get one later, you'll have the public-speaking experience to handle it. If you work in a contentious field, we suggest reading Weissman's (2005) book; it explains how to handle the bone-jarring, blistering questions that occur in high-stakes public speaking.

You will, however, meet many sincere, cheerful, and clueless questioners, people who ask weird questions that make no sense to you or to the rest of audience. (For examples, see Paul's Woeful Tale of Woe.) Perhaps we are stereotyping, but we suspect that having incomprehensible questions correlates highly with having the impulsive urge to blurt things out in front of large groups. People with weird questions can't inhibit them. Weird questions often stem from poor social skills: inappropriate self-disclosure, poor turn-taking, or the compulsion to speak after sitting quietly for 45 minutes.

Quirky questions deserve the same consideration and grace as normal questions—don't be haughty or dramatic. Your audience is perplexed by the question, too, so they're curious to how you respond. If you have experience teaching college courses, you already have the skills to handle odd questions. Our approach has three prongs.

First, look for the grain of a good idea in the question. Few questions are wildly off; there's usually some way to bring a question back on track. For example, you can elaborate a small part of the question or reframe the question in terms of your topic:

- "Your remark about [tiny comprehensible kernel in the otherwise bizarre question], in particular, is interesting."

I confess to no truly woeful tales of woe involving questions. In my years of public speaking, I haven't had question-and-answer disasters. In fact, I enjoy fielding questions more than giving the prepared talk. But I've been asked a lot of comical questions. Here's a sample, reworded for clarity, such as it is:

- "Hmm, do you think interest might be an emotion?" (This question was asked after a 45-minute talk titled *Interest: The Curious Emotion,* in which I argued that interest should be considered an emotion.)
- "What does this work have to do with developing innovative household products for the blind?" (I can't explain—you had to be there.)
- "I study long-distance cyclists—I mean, *really* long distance— they're incredible athletes, just incredible. I don't know how they do it. Anyway, what does your work have to do with that? Anything?" (The talk was about causal attribution in a sample of college students.)
- "What if you used multilevel finite mixture models?" (In fairness, this was in response to my saying, "Phew, I'm glad no one asked about the multilevel finite mixture models.")
- "Do you really have a wallaby stashed in the rafters?" (No one has asked this yet, but I suspect that a reader of this book will, just to be a smart-ass.)

- What you're asking, I think, is [not exactly what the person asked, but close], and that's an interesting problem."

This is easier said than done, of course; it will take some practice. If there's a silver lining, it's that these questioners appear to be content with any answer. Just as they don't see the irrelevance of their questions to your talk, they won't see the irrelevance of your answer to their questions. The sword of weirdness cuts both ways.

Second, you can ask the questioner for more detail. If flabbergasted, simply say, "I'm not sure what you mean. Could you expand on that a bit?" The extra information might give you fodder for an answer. If you're lucky, the person will offer a few broken sentences, sputter, and say, "Oh, never mind. I'm not sure—I need to think about it some more." People sometimes get confused by their own questions.

Third, it's okay to say, "I don't know; that's a tricky one. Let's chat about it after the talk." This is public speaking's nuclear option, so don't use it more than once per talk. A speaker can get away with only one flagrant dodge.

ASKING QUESTIONS

Learning how to field questions will make you a better audience member. After a few talks, you'll have a new appreciation for the art of asking good questions. At a minimum, don't be mean, and don't ask a question that lacks an answer. For example, there's no good answer to "Have you considered using a zero-inflated negative binomial model here?" And avoid, if you can, questions born of compulsion and affectation. For example, we've known grad students who asked "What about gender differences?" at every talk, regardless of the topic. Other students would do impressions of them, in that Saroyanesque manner in which grad students mock each other. (Other people opt for "cultural differences," a variant form.) Your compulsive question may be a great question, but it will get old quickly, and people will be too annoyed to notice its value.

Ponderous Reflections and Conclusions

If you lack the "gift of gab"—formally known as *high verbal fluency* or *bullshitting* (Frankfurt, 2005)—you can nevertheless learn to handle questions well. Avoiding defensiveness is a good start. If nothing else, you can convey openness and sincerity. But with some practice, you'll be able to think nimbly on your feet. You'll know that you're a pro when you hear "Good job—my work is done here" whispered from the rafters.

5

Managing Anxiety

Anxiety is evolution's way of keeping us safe. If your ancient cousin Ug were gathering berries and encountered a grizzly bear, it would behoove him to be afraid. The ramped-up response of his autonomic nervous system would allow him to fight or flee the situation. But anxiety isn't as useful when delivering a talk, unless, of course, you're talking to an audience of bears (not those eucalyptus-eating marsupial imposters, mind you; the real thing).

If you were invited to speak to a bunch of bears, you might refuse, procrastinate, anticipate disaster, even decide to back out at the last minute—all ways anxiety hurts the planning and delivery of a presentation. Although you're not speaking to bears, some part of you may interpret the situation as equally dangerous: You might believe the audience is judging you harshly, you'll pass out at any moment, or you'll embarrass yourself in some horrible way. These anticipated disasters are the real bears. Fortunately, they're probably not objectively dangerous, mostly because they lack scary, pointy teeth. Think of them as teddy bears that look incredibly real. In this chapter, we'll show you how to beat these cute little guys to a pulp using four effective tools: careful practice, mental imagery, relaxation training, and self-talk strategies.

You've probably heard that mild anxiety is a good thing. According to the classic Yerkes–Dodson law of "optimal arousal" (Yerkes & Dodson, 1908), high levels of arousal interfere with performance. All of us have experienced times when we were so nervous we couldn't think. Panic attacks aren't exactly famous for focusing our attention on the task at hand. Then again, very low levels of arousal aren't very helpful either. Although low levels of anxiety are probably better than panic levels, being too relaxed doesn't provide sufficient motivation for performing well. Moderate arousal probably leads to the best performance. When you're a little nervous, your brain seems to fire on all cylinders, your attention is focused on the task at hand, and you're motivated to perform well.

So, our goal in this chapter is to help you manage your anxiety, not remove it altogether. As Freud once put it, "A certain degree of neurosis is of inestimable value as a drive, especially to a psychologist." He also said, "Time spent with cats is never wasted." He was a great man.

CAREFUL PREPARATION AND PRACTICE

When it comes time to give their presentation, many people with public-speaking anxiety feel that they're "not ready." Even after delivering dozens of talks, Dave and Paul sometimes still feel unprepared at the moment it's time to speak. Most of the time, people who feel this way actually are ready, but their negative self-talk is getting the better of them. We'll discuss how to combat such distorted thoughts later. For now, if you really think you're not ready, there's a simple solution: Get ready. Spend more time preparing and practicing.

We've already said a lot in Chapter 3 about preparation and practice. At the risk of boring you, we'll reiterate two important tips here. First, good presentations begin with good planning. You're likely to feel less nervous when you've carefully organized and written your talk. If you're afraid that you'll forget your talking points, make a set of simple notes. The key word here is *simple*. Notes should be easy to follow. We recommend writing a one- to two-page outline of your talk, not a full script. An uncomplicated outline will jog your memory without tempting you to simply read from notes. If your notes are cleanly organized, you're also less likely to lose your place. Well-organized PowerPoint slides also can serve as notes to help you remember what to talk about next.

Second, it's important to practice your talk several times. The more practice you've done, the more prepared you'll feel and the better you're likely to perform. The idea is to overlearn your talk. In a nutshell, overlearning means learning your presentation better than you need to. A great way to combat anxiety is to practice your talk so many times that you give it in your sleep. (For once, you'll be thankful that your roommate films you while you sleep.) The reason for overlearning is simple: Research on social facilitation shows that anxiety is less likely to interfere with well-learned tasks (Zajonc, 1965). A two-step process for effective practice can be found in Chapter 3.

Imagery Exercises

Another strategy for reducing your anxiety and improving your performance involves positive mental imagery. Technically known as *mental simulation*, this process involves the cognitive representation of an event or series of events. Basically, it's like practicing in your mind. With your eyes closed, you envision doing the behavior you plan to perform. A good deal of research demonstrates that this technique can improve outcomes as well as increase self-efficacy and behavioral intentions (Anderson 1983; Felz & Landers, 1983; Taylor & Pham, 1999). Although actual practice is clearly better than mental practice alone, a combination of the two may be particularly powerful (Felz & Landers, 1983).

Here's a simple method for doing your own mental simulation:

- First, make sure you've got a basic working knowledge of what's in your talk. Although you don't have to know the entire talk word for word, you should have enough of your talk written to be able to envision yourself giving it.
- Second, make a script for your mental simulation. Divide a clean sheet of paper into two columns.

On the left, write at least three things that you fear might occur during your talk. Think of these as obstacles that might get in the way of doing perfectly. It's important to make these obstacles realistic. As discussed in Chapter 6, it's probably realistic to think that your PowerPoint slides might not load correctly, whereas it's unrealistic to expect the audience to pee on you. After you've determined three obstacles, use the right column to record how you could realistically deal with each of these obstacles.

- Third, close your eyes and begin your imagery exercise. There are a couple of things to keep in mind here. It's very important to make the imagery as detailed as possible. Use all five senses; look around and notice where you are, what the room looks like, what the temperature is, what you hear, and any smell in the air. Of equal importance, the imagery should be realistic. In other words, don't allow yourself to spiral off into unlikely worst-case scenarios or, alternatively, happy rainbows-and-kittens fantasies. Instead, picture how the scene actually would go.

- Last, use your script with the three obstacles. See yourself beginning the talk, then successfully dealing with each obstacle as it occurs. Practice the scene from beginning to end, walking through each step along the way; don't just skip to the part where you finish. Finally, see yourself completing the talk and feeling good about it.

When you finish the exercise, consider if you'd like to revise the script or the imagery in any way. Then, do it again. Repeat this process at least twice a week until you give your talk. You'll probably feel a bit more confident each time you work through the scene. By the way, given that you've imagined three obstacles occurring during your talk, this is likely to be close to a worst-case scenario. Although this many problems can occur, it's highly unlikely. But it wasn't so bad, was it?

RELAXATION TRAINING

Progressive muscle relaxation (PMR; Jacobson, 1938) offers another method for reducing anxiety. As you probably know, research has demonstrated that there is an emotional feedback loop between the brain and body (LeDoux, 1996; Schachter & Singer, 1962). Although researchers debate the specifics, they generally agree that we feel emotions at least partly in our body. When you experience unpleasant emotions, your heart rate can increase; your breathing may change; and most important, your muscles often tense. This physical tension then feeds back to modulate your emotional experience. The more your muscles tense, the more anxious you'll probably feel. On the other hand, if you can find a way to decrease muscular tension, your anxiety will likely decrease. That's where PMR comes in.

- Start by finding a quiet place. You can do this exercise sitting, lying down, or hanging like a bat from the ceiling. If you're likely to fall asleep, however, lying down may not be the best choice. Get comfortable, close your eyes, and take a few deep breaths.

■ Focus your attention on your hands. Tense your hands by making them into fists. Fully experience the tension, but don't squeeze so tightly that you hurt yourself. After a few seconds, release the muscles and allow your fingers to spread out comfortably.

■ Now shift your attention to your wrists. Tense your wrists by bending your hands back so that your fingers are pointed toward the ceiling. Experience the tension for a few seconds, then let go. Enjoy the relaxed feeling in your hands and wrists for a few moments before moving on.

■ Continue this process for each of the major parts of your body, one by one, including your biceps, shoulders, forehead, jaw, lips, neck, chest and stomach, buttocks, thighs, shins, and feet. Tense each body part for a few seconds, then loosen the muscles and enjoy the relaxation for a moment before moving on.

■ If you want to feel really New Age, try envisioning a warm glow encompassing each part of your body as you tense and relax. As this light touches each muscle, see its warmth dissolving any tension present. When you're finished with the exercise, spend a few minutes with your eyes closed and enjoy the warmth and relaxation spreading through your body.

If possible, put down the book and try this exercise now. It should take 15 to 20 minutes if done at a moderately slow, calming pace. If you find it helpful, consider practicing two or three times a week until your talk. Each time, you'll notice that the relaxation occurs more rapidly and fully. Eventually, you may be able to combine groups of muscles, so you're tensing and relaxing your upper body all at once, followed by your lower body. After a while, you might even find that you can quit the tensing part all together; instead, simply close your eyes for a minute and envision the warm, relaxing glow encompassing your body.

Once you get the hang of it, try using this technique just before delivering your presentation. Chances are, you'll feel more relaxed and focused as a result. It's best to find a secluded place to do this, such as a conference hotel room or restroom. Although some hotels boast excellent rafters, we recommend reserving the bat approach for home—a you-know-what might be stashed there.

SELF-TALK STRATEGIES

We all have a monologue running just below the mental surface. It's as if we've got little sports commentators following us around. They comment on the way we look, how we act, even who we are. When people experience public-speaking anxiety, it's typically because these commentators have turned nasty. As psychologists are wont to do, there is a proliferation of names for these fleeting interpretations of events. They've been called *automatic thoughts* (Beck, 1979), *irrational beliefs* (Ellis, 1999), and even *covert behaviors* (Skinner, 1971).

They range from fairly harmless thoughts such as "Is my fly down?" to more damaging statements like "Everyone thinks I'm stupid."

Although most of us experience at least occasional negative self-talk when performing in front of others, some people take these statements seriously whereas others disregard them, especially when they're not realistic. In fact, our self-talk can be downright distorted and irrational. Your fly probably isn't down; most likely people don't think you're stupid. Do you really believe the audience is that mean?

- The first step in combating negative self-talk is tuning into it. A useful exercise involves dividing a clean sheet of paper into three columns. In the first column, write down all the negative thoughts you experience while delivering presentations. You've probably already got some idea of what you typically say to yourself when speaking in front of others. If you have trouble identifying your negative thoughts, however, try practicing your talk in front of others. That'll get the self-talk going. Negative self-talk also often arises during the imagery exercise detailed earlier in the chapter.
- Next, consider how these thoughts might be distorted or unrealistic. Exhibit 5.1 contains a list of cognitive distortions. Although you've probably seen longer lists than this one (J. S. Beck, 1995; Burns, 1999), in our experience, these are the distortions that most commonly afflict people with

EXHIBIT 5.1 Common Cognitive Distortions in
Public-Speaking Anxiety

- **All-or-Nothing Thinking:** You evaluate things in black-or-white extremes—either you did perfectly on your presentation or you absolutely sucked. You miss the shades of gray between these extremes.
- **Catastrophizing:** Without any evidence, you're sure that the worst possible outcome of your talk will occur. This is sometimes called the "Fortune-Telling Error."
- **Emotional Reasoning:** You assume that your feelings are an accurate indication of reality. Because you *feel* uncomfortable during or after your talk, you assume it must have gone badly.
- **Magnification and Minimization:** You blow small negative aspects of your performance out of proportion ("I can't believe my nose kept running during the talk!") and overlook or discount larger positive aspects ("Audiences give lots of people standing ovations").
- **Mind Reading:** You're certain of what other people are thinking about you and your performance even though you have no evidence.
- **Personalization:** You assume that something is about you when it really isn't. If the projector breaks down and your talk suffers as a result, you blame yourself.

public-speaking anxiety. Our favorite is mind reading. Novice presenters do this all the time. You might find yourself thinking, "Everyone knows this is my first presentation," "The audience can tell I'm nervous," or even, "They all think I'm an idiot." How do you know? Despite popular belief, psychologists aren't psychic (except you, of course). Use the second column of your worksheet to write down which cognitive distortions correspond to each negative thought. Don't make the mistake of confusing your thoughts with reality. In other words, don't believe everything you think. See Dave's Woeful Tale of Woe for the perils of doing this.

Dave's Woeful Tale of Woe

A few years ago, I had the opportunity to do my first public therapy demonstration. Although I already had given numerous talks, the prospect of conducting psychotherapy in front of an audience frightened me. What if the client is resistant, belligerent, or even angry? What if the therapy just doesn't work? My self-talk included such winners as, "Everyone's going to see I'm a fraud"; "I just know I'll screw up"; and even, "I hope I don't get fired over this." These fears were unfounded, especially because it wasn't even a real client or real therapy, but a demonstration with a student volunteer who was coached beforehand. Nonetheless, my self-talk got the better of me. Being a good little soldier, I did the demonstration anyway.

Predictably, I was anxious during the entire demonstration. Afterward, I continued to beat myself up viciously with self-talk statements like, "See! I screwed it up," and "That truly sucked." That night, I went home feeling depressed and dejected.

Luckily, I tore myself away from the pity party long enough to check my e-mail inbox, which contained a message from the chair of my department. Here's what it said: "I expected to see an excellent therapist, but what I saw reflected sensitivity and skill beyond your years." What happened, you ask? I made the mistake of believing my self-talk. Rather than looking at the situation objectively and truly seeing that I performed reasonably well, I let my distorted interpretations run away with me.

In retrospect, this isn't much of a tale of woe. It's actually a pretty positive story. Nonetheless, if that e-mail hadn't been there, who knows if I ever would have realized I did a good job?

- Use the third column to respond to your distorted thoughts. Now that you know which distortions you're using, write down a more rational way of talking to yourself. If you have trouble thinking of a rational response, try asking yourself, "If a close friend experienced these distorted thoughts, what would I say to him or her?" Make sure that your rational responses aren't overly positive. You're probably not going to wow your audience so much that they shower you with hundred-dollar bills. Nonetheless, you might get through your talk without any big mistakes. For a rational response to calm your nerves, it should be more plausible than your distorted belief.

- Now look at your worksheet and see if you can boil down all of your rational responses to a short, reassuring, and realistic statement. You might end up with something like, "Even though sometimes you think you suck, you really don't"; "There's no way of knowing what the audience thinks"; or "I'm my own worst critic, but chances are I'm going to do pretty well."

If you begin unfairly criticizing yourself during the talk, use the statement you just crafted to combat your anxiety. Simply pause for a moment and remind yourself of this rational response. The audience won't even notice you're doing it. Then, shift your attention to the task at hand. Rather than focusing on thoughts of doom and gloom, concentrate on what you're speaking about. Instead of thinking, "My talk sucks," ask yourself, "How can I best meet the needs of my audience at this moment?" With a little practice, your self-talk can work for rather than against you.

WHEN TO SEEK HELP

Throughout this chapter, we've assumed that your anxiety is normal and manageable without psychotherapy. Sometimes, however, anxiety rises to the point that it's difficult to manage without therapy. If your field is clinical or counseling psychology, you probably already have considered this. For our nonclinician readers, here are three ways to know if professional help is called for.

First, anxiety can interfere with functioning. Chances are you're reading this because nervousness affects your ability to speak in public. That's true for most of us. Nonetheless, most people can get through their talk and do an adequate job despite such feelings. If you're not able to go on, can't get through your talk, or avoid public speaking altogether, you should consider seeking professional help, especially if these symptoms affect your career.

Second, you've tried managing the anxiety on your own and it hasn't worked. Provided that you've already given the techniques in this chapter a fair try, you should consider consulting with a professional, especially if the symptoms are causing you distress or annoyance. Psychotherapists can offer a variety of effective methods, such as exposure therapy and cognitive restructuring (Kozasa & Leite, 1998), which could potentially reduce your anxiety significantly after only a few sessions.

Third, you just want some extra help. Therapy can be a rewarding and pampering experience. Why go it on your own if you can afford an expert? Although not everyone feels this way, many do. If you find yourself desiring the help of a professional, it's probably not a bad idea.

PONDEROUS REFLECTIONS AND CONCLUSIONS

We're convinced that the tools in this chapter will reduce your fear of public speaking. The key is to use these techniques consistently during the weeks leading up to your talk. If you start now, when you get up to the podium, you could look out at an audience of teddy bears rather than vicious grizzlies. Just avoid the urge to cuddle; that might freak somebody out.

6

When Disaster Strikes: Handling Problems With Humor and Grace

In the middle of my talk, Something Bad will happen. To fear public speaking is to fear disaster, to fear that something will go horribly awry during your talk. If public speaking doesn't bother you, you won't know what we mean. But if public speaking makes you anxious, you understand. Vague, global fears are hallmarks of anxiety. The fear of Something Bad, like all vague fears, deserves a closer look: What specific public-speaking disasters might befall us?

We could die, of course. It could happen. One moment we're in the middle of describing a slide, bravely stammering through a bulleted list, and whammo: We crumple to the ground, small Xs over our eyes, a laser pointer clutched in one hand. A grad student jumps up and shouts "Is there a doctor in the house?" (Realizing his folly, he adds "I mean a real doctor, not the PhD kind.") Dying midtalk is unlikely, but it does have its comforts. If you fear public speaking, then dying is one way to get out of the talk and to avoid the question-and-answer period. It's also one of the few ways to get people to remember your talk. We remember only a handful of the hundreds of brief presentations we've seen: Most were merely deadly boring, not actually deadly. And your posthumous reputation as a speaker will be enhanced. Years later, people will say "She was hard-core—the paramedics had to rip the laser pointer out of her cold, dead hand."

But dying midtalk is unlikely. Many other disasters, however, are waiting to happen. One day, for example, koalas and wallabies will set aside their differences and rise up against us. They will storm the exhibit hall, knocking over the poster boards, smearing the exhibitors' booths with wallaby dung and half-chewed eucalyptus leaves. Only the hirsute and Psi Chi members will be spared. Will you be ready?

Perhaps you don't fear koalas and wallabies, having sensibly avoided conferences in Australia. Your fear could be more prosaic, such as peeing your pants. This could be embarrassing, we suppose, but it's unlikely: You have a greater chance of being peed on by someone else. Be wary of anyone sitting in the front row—like our students, we would rather sit in the back, where we can gossip about the speakers and take nips of espresso from our jacket flasks. If someone in the front is drinking from a gallon-sized water bottle, stand behind the podium—it's as good of a shield as you'll find.

More seriously, some people fear medical emergencies while speaking. Some pregnant women worry about going into labor; people with epilepsy worry about having a seizure; people with migraines worry about crippling headaches; people with serious allergies worry about allergen exposure in the haphazard environment of a conference. These worries are serious and realistic. Fortunately, rare things happen rarely. Unless you have a good reason to fear mortality, marsupials, or micturition, they won't happen. And if an emergency strikes, you won't care about your trivial talk. True emergencies put your talk—and the quaint, fuzzy fears that most people call disasters—in perspective. If you go into labor during your talk, just announce "I'm going into labor, so I'm so out of here—see you at next year's meeting. And don't steal my damn laser pointer."

Most of public speaking's quirks and hitches can be prevented. This chapter describes how to avoid public speaking's most common problems. Over a long career, you'll run into all of them: They happen all the time. Some public-speaking problems can't be prevented—random things happen randomly—but you can learn tricks for managing them when they happen. Even epic, dinosaur-killing disasters can be handled with humor and grace—unless you're a stegosaurus, of course.

THE AUDIENCE IS YOUR FRIEND

The key to managing calamity is to understand that the audience is on your side. They may be bored and listless during your talk, but they'll side with you if something goes wrong. Psychologists tend to be sympathetic, play-well-with-others types: It's one of many traits that is highly correlated with listening to National Public Radio and frequenting farmer's markets. And most of your audience gives talks, too, so they know that things go awry. If you simply make a joke and move on, people will respect you for your poise. But if you curse, fret, or get flustered, you'll lose your audience's sympathy. "Get over it," they'll think. "It isn't that big of a deal."

Consider, for example, two ways of handling a midtalk calamity. Just as you reach the dramatic denouement—will it be statistically significant?—the projector flickers and dies. Computer projectors are fickle beasts, animated by a cruel desire to thwart your SEPA talk. You could curse under your breath—or loudly— and spend a few minutes tinkering desperately with the machine, trying to revive it. This is the bad, graceless way. The audience can see that you're stressed. Each passing minute makes you more stressed and the audience more impatient. When you finally give up and say, "Okay, let's just keep going," you'll hear exasperated sighs and grumbles of "it's about time" from the audience. Trying to salvage the talk made it awkward.

Instead, just make a joke and move on. Any joke will do: The goal is to handle the event with humor, poise, and grace. You could make a self-deprecating joke ("Wow, even the projector is bored by my talk"), a non sequitur ("I knew I should have showered"), or a joke about the crappy equipment ("Should we have a moment of silence for the expired projector?"). The point is to convey that it isn't a big deal, that you won't be derailed. Then finish your talk, take questions, and sit down. From the audience's perspective, you took the hitch in stride. They'll giggle at your joke, sympathize with your plight, and appreciate that you soldiered on. If you aren't funny, don't worry. Many psychologists—perhaps millions—are not even slightly funny. You can omit the joke part and simply move on.

People watching your talk are like toddlers who whomp into a coffee table. Slightly confused, they look at you to see if what happened merits crying or giggling. The audience won't make a big deal out of a disaster if you don't.

PREVENTING AND MANAGING PREDICTABLE DISASTERS

Technical Problems

Technology can be dangerous. Conferences lack a standard for equipment. You can usually, but not always, use your own notebook computer. Sometimes, the session moderator provides the computer; other times, the conference provides computers, which might belong to the venue, the conference organizers, a local college, or a company that rents equipment. If the computers come from the venue or a rental business, they're probably old, crusty, and stripped down. They will have Microsoft PowerPoint but not much else.

You never know what you'll be stuck with. The computer might be too old: We've seen conference computers that lack USB ports and wireless antennas, making it impossible to use a file from a USB drive or from e-mail. Conversely, the computer might be too new: It could have a snazzy new operating system that won't read your file. Or the computer simply might be the wrong kind: The small but valiant cadre of Mac users know what we mean. The computer may work initially, only to suddenly update, restart, or run diagnostics during your presentation.

If you think computers are rancorous, you won't like computer projectors. Projecting an image onto a screen, in principle, should be easy: You connect the computer and projector, the computer sends stuff to the projector, the projector heats up to a near-volcanic temperature, and a bulleted list appears. But projectors fail all the time. Conference projectors are usually owned by the conference venue (e.g., the hotel) or rented from the same guys who provided the crusty notebook computers. We suspect that they own crappy projectors to prevent theft by sticky-fingered koalas.

If the computer and projector are fine, you can still have a file-format disaster. As discussed in Chapter 3, most people use Microsoft PowerPoint to make their slides. This is good because you can be certain that the conference computer will have PowerPoint. If you use OpenOffice Impress or Corel Presentations, we can appreciate your willingness to go against the grain, to show that you're an individual who individually expresses your individuality. But individuality goes before a fall—to wit, see Paul's Woeful Tale of Woe.

My first conference talk had a comical slide show meltdown. This disaster's origins stretch deep into my past, to my adolescent preference for WordPerfect over Word. Because I used the Corel WordPerfect suite of programs, not Microsoft Office, I always made my course lectures in Corel Presentations and exported them to "Show-on-the-Go" format, a self-executing slide presentation that would ostensibly run on any machine. When I made my slides for the conference talk, I did the same thing. What could go wrong?

During my talk, I noticed that the uncommon characters were rendered as weird icons, like smiley faces and diacritical marks. The text was grainy, too, like an old Atari 2600 game. And in the middle of the talk, I noticed that the Results slide had vanished. This was bad: the missing slide had two bar charts and some descriptive statistics, the core of the talk. Because it was my first presentation, I was not yet skilled in the dark art of self-deprecating quips. Nevertheless, I moved on, pointing out that a slide was missing and describing the results of the study. Then I quipped, "That's the last time I'll use Corel Presentations instead of PowerPoint." And it was.

Perhaps you can't access your slides at all. It's wise to bring your slides on a USB flash drive, but flash drives are fickle. You might lose it while traveling, sit on it, or drop it into a cup of coffee. Your drive may simply choose that day to fail. The computer may lack a USB port, an increasingly unlikely possibility. "Phew! I saved it in my e-mail account," you think. That's wise, too, but you might not be able to access the Internet on short notice. Conference hotels often lack free wireless access to the Internet, and the room's computer may not be connected to the Internet.

In ancient times, people prevented technical disasters by bringing overhead transparencies as backups, affectionately known as *overheads*. We feel a bittersweet nostalgia when we realize that the latest generation of researchers will never use these quaint artifacts. Conferences used to have overhead projectors sitting in the corner, ready to leap into loud, dusty action if the computer failed. Those were more innocent times. Today, few conferences have overhead backups—too few people use them, and they're expensive. A few conferences still offer overhead projectors, but not enough do for us to recommend bringing overheads as backups. So if the equipment fails, you'll experience the greatest dinosaur-killing cataclysm of them all: no projector, no computer, and no chalkboard.

If an unforeseen calamity strikes, fear not. You have two options. First, you can unleash your old-school skills: Just stand there and talk. It sounds bizarre, almost subversive in its Luddism, but it works. Second, you can bring handouts. Print four or six slides per page, make a bunch of copies, and hand them out to the audience if necessary. We suspect that experienced speakers will prefer the first option: If you feel comfortable winging it, then there's no need to carry handouts to the conference. But if you're new to speaking and you fear technical disasters, then a file folder of photocopies will make you feel better.

These technical problems will happen to everyone eventually, but most of them can be prevented. First, save your slides in PowerPoint for PC format, preferably in several places. It's rare that your USB drive, your friend's USB drive, a CD, *and* your e-mail account will fail you. Second, show up at least 15 minutes early for your talk. This gives you time to load your file on the machine, to click through the slides, and to see how they look when projected.

Time Problems

You often won't have as much time as you expected. This disaster is the common cold of conference life. Psychologists talk too much as it is: When you give them an audience they'll ramble on and on, adding caveats, describing fascinating implications, and declaring that each question is an interesting one. Talking too long cuts into other speakers' time: This is why we call it a cardinal sin of public speaking (see Chapter 2). If a session's moderator is reluctant to intervene, the last speaker in a session of six talks is screwed. (Most moderators, however, are quick with the vaudeville hook, so don't worry if you're last.) Rarely, a last-minute schedule change will cut into your time: Instead of 60 minutes, you might have 30; instead of 20 minutes, you might have 10.

You may be tempted to collapse—"But I rehearsed that talk 12 times. It's exactly 20 minutes!"—but this is an easy problem to fix. First, as we said in Chapter 2, you should plan a time buffer into your talk. If you have 20 minutes, plan for 15. Second, talk less. If you have a few minutes to prepare, shave a slide or two from your slide show and delete some text from each slide. If you don't have time to trim the slides, just skip over the unimportant ideas and slides. Everything seems important when you have a lot of time; a time crunch will make your talk sleeker.

Talking less is harder than it sounds. Don't complain about the lack of time, and resist the urge to make snarky, frustrated jokes at the garrulous person's expense. The audience is on your side. They know that it's hard to compress a talk, and they know the other speaker ripped you off. They'll think badly of the other speaker on your behalf, so leave it alone. If you pick on the other person, you'll lose the audience's goodwill. Just move on. You can get your revenge later—just slip a few eucalyptus leaves in the person's jacket and let the koalas do your dirty work.

Audience Problems

Occasionally, no one shows up. No one. This happened to Paul once. (Dave, in contrast, is far too cool to be stiffed this way.) During a day of meetings and workshops, he hit a dead spot: Not a single person came to a slot reserved for talking with grad students, who had a class at that time. If you think about it, this isn't a problem—just go get coffee, take a bathroom break, or clean the eucalyptus stains from your shirt. It's much more awkward when just a handful of people show up. This rarely happens at conferences. When it does, it usually happens at the first and last sessions, when people are traveling to and from the conference. But a small audience isn't a problem—just give your talk to the people who took the time to show up.

More troubling are irascible and confusing audience members. You may have a peevish know-it-all in the audience, someone who asks mean-spirited questions, questions without answers, or monologues disguised as questions. Having read Chapter 4, you already know how to handle these people, and you know that they're rare in psychology.

MANAGING UNPREDICTABLE, DINOSAUR-KILLING DISASTERS

So far, we've covered nearly all of the predictable public-speaking problems you'll experience during your long, happy career. They're easy to anticipate, to prevent, and to manage. Unpredictable calamities, however, are a different beast: You never know what will happen. We've seen and faced some weird problems.

A few years ago, Paul gave a research talk at a small conference in Florida. Midtalk, loud, tacky country music started playing in the next room. The hotel was setting up for a wedding reception to celebrate two peoples' love for each other and for bad music. It was hilarious. One moment, the audience was deep in consternated boredom; the next moment, Shania Twain's

"You're The One" was playing at 85 decibels. Applying the "make a joke and move on" principle, Paul made a lame joke (something like "I can't believe it—I left North Carolina to escape country music") and kept going. After Shania, DJ Hotelier played ABBA's "Dancing Queen," which complemented the mixed-model ANOVAs nicely. Paul wrapped up the talk, the audience didn't ask questions, and the experience faded into the hazy realm of "it will make a good story someday."

Since his ABBA talk, Paul has learned that wedding–conference clashes are common. A couple years later, he saw a hotel stop a poster session to make room for a reception. The weddings usually win. We suspect that it's harder to palliate "You ruined our wedding" than "You ruined my talk about personality predictors of smoking cessation attempts in a sample of at-risk rural youth." The point, though, is that you can't predict or prevent such a thing. Just make a joke and move on.

Dave saw a bizarre talk at the Midwestern Psychological Association conference many years ago. The speaker—a well-known, widely traveled clinical psychologist—was fielding questions when a graduate student asked him an odd question about assessment, noting that he had done some research on the matter. The student then asked, "Can I tell you about it sometime?"; the speaker—obviously thinking that *sometime* didn't mean *immediately*—said "Sure." The student then stood up, whipped out some overheads, and gave a brief presentation to the startled audience. We don't know who that student was, but we would like to know. (If it was you, you're an idiot.)

So how do you handle unpredictable calamities like talk usurpers? The speaker did the best thing he could do: He shrugged it off and moved on. We would have been tempted to ridicule the guy, or at least to menace him with the business end of the laser pointer. But the speaker played it well. The audience had already rightfully condemned the student—it's a terrible violation of conference norms, and the audience is on the speaker's side—and people with real questions deserved the remaining time.

PONDEROUS REFLECTIONS AND CONCLUSIONS

You can't prevent the unpredictable disasters, but you can prevent the easy stuff. And the true disasters will never happen. You won't die, koalas won't attack you, the people in the front row won't pee on you. But the koalas might—bring an umbrella, just in case.

II

HELP WITH SPECIFIC
PRESENTATIONS

7

Research Talks

Of the many behaviors of *Studentus Backward-Hatticus*—the common North American college student—the most perplexing is the refusal to do any assigned reading. College students are a black hole of literacy. Even the shortest and most lively article is too long and boring for them to read; if it wasn't posted 10 minutes ago on the Internet, they don't want to see it. We often act baffled at their behavior. If you've read this far, however, we know you well enough to confess to professorial hypocrisy. Like our students, we like to sit in the back, to check e-mail every 90 seconds, and even occasionally to wear hats backwards. If possible, we'd rather not read the interminable articles that clog our professional journals.

This is one reason why we love research talks. Instead of reading, we can sit in the back of the room, turn our hats backwards, and passively absorb the latest research. In this chapter, we'll describe how to give psychology's favorite talk: the 15-minute conference presentation. Many people's first professional presentation is a short research talk at a regional conference. This is good. You don't want your debut to be a job talk, an hour-long invited address, or a morning-long testimony to a congressional subcommittee. Brief research talks are psychology's bread and butter (or bread and Vegemite at Australian conferences), and nearly all of the field's presentation genres are based on the basic principles we'll cover in this chapter.

If you've never attended a conference before, we recommend starting with a poster (see Chapter 8), not a talk. It's helpful to attend a handful of talks before actually giving one. We understand, though, that not everyone can do this. You might have been invited to give a talk, and it would be awkward to decline, or your pushy advisor may believe that skipping posters will build character. Regardless, this chapter will get you started.

GETTING YOUR PRESENTATION ACCEPTED AT A CONFERENCE

Conferences are swamped with people who want to present—there isn't room for everyone. We'd like to think that the urge to communicate exciting discoveries to cherished colleagues is the reason, but we suspect that for many, it's more about getting a free trip. To manage the chaos, conference planners reserve a few big slots for famous people and a lot of small slots for the rest of us. A regional conference, for example, might have six hour-long talks but 150 fifteen-minute ones. These short talks are grouped into sessions by topic, saving the audience the trouble of moving from room to room.

To give one of these talks, you must submit an abstract. Conferences release a "Call for Papers" or "Call for Submissions" about 9 months before the conference. The call specifies a due date, the kinds of presentations you can apply to give (e.g., brief talks, posters, workshops), the information you must provide, and the format of the abstract. Read these guidelines carefully because they can differ widely from conference to conference.

There are two rules for these abstracts: (a) Turn the thing in on time, and (b) follow the format guidelines. To understand why these rules are inviolable, it helps to learn how conference abstracts are evaluated. Paul and Dave have judged submissions for several conferences, and it always happens the same way: As a favor to a friend (i.e., you owe someone) or as a service to the profession (i.e., you're going up for promotion), you agree to evaluate submissions for a conference. "How bad can it be?" you think. A few months later, you feel like a gullible moron when you receive a monstrous stack of submissions. You regret agreeing to judge them; your wallaby assistant, moreover, stokes the flames of resentment by snickering and coughing "Ahem, ahem, loser, ahem."

Imagine that people submitted 65 abstracts to you: How would you evaluate them? If there are only 50 slots, you must reject 15 people. The first cut involves rejecting everything that came in late. It's unfair to people who followed the rules to accept a late talk in favor of an on-time talk, so the latecomers get rejected. "The axe!" you shout, and your furry, four-pawed assistant fires off rejection e-mails to the procrastinators. This eliminates five abstracts—only 10 more to go. The second cut eliminates everything that fails to follow the guidelines: submissions that are too long, too short, improperly formatted, and so on. So the improper submissions get the axe next—this eliminates eight. Perfect—you chopped 13 submissions without even reading them, and the rest of the rejections can be based on substantive reasons.

Turning in a late or shoddy abstract is like begging for rejection. If you give your abstract the attention it deserves, however, your chances will be pretty good. For large conferences, around half of the proposals are accepted. For many small conferences, though, no one is rejected for substantive reasons—everyone who took the trouble to turn in a good abstract is rewarded with a spot.

WHAT SHOULD YOU EMPHASIZE? WHAT SHOULD YOU SKIP?

For a 15-minute talk, you'll have 12 minutes for your talk and 3 minutes for questions. Compressing your brilliant research into a 12-minute space is hard—you'll have to leave a lot out, and it isn't in the anal-retentive nature of scientists to leave things out. During your talk, you should emphasize information that helps people understand what you did, what you found, and why it's important. Most of your audience will never read the article based on your talk, so this is your chance to convey the basic ideas behind your work.

You can use the elements of an APA Style article as a guide. Your talk will have an Introduction, a Method section, a Results section, and a Discussion. Here are a few tips to guide your writing:

- For the Introduction, describe the motivation behind the work. How does it fit in the stream of thought on the topic? What is the biggest new contribution of the research? Why is it worth 15 minutes of your audience's life?
- For the Method section, describe the most important aspects of the sample and procedures. Who participated? How did you manipulate or assess your variables? Is there something novel—a new task, measure, or procedure—that needs extra attention?
- For the Results section, describe the major findings. Did you find what you predicted? If possible, display your findings visually (see Chapter 3).
- For the Discussion, the shortest part, describe your take-home message. The Introduction was only a few minutes ago, so your audience will remember the work's background and motivation. Conclude your talk with one or two major implications: Brief is good.

You should skip the details that are best left to published articles. Some information is important but overly technical. For example, in an article you can explore every obscure implication of your research. Your readers want to know this stuff, but your listeners have time for only one or two big implications. Likewise, articles often have long sections devoted to limitations, science's version of ritual self-flagellation. Such exercises in modesty are fine in an article, but you don't have time for them in your 12-minute talk. If your research has profound, fatal flaws, then you are either brave or clueless for giving a talk about it. But if your work has only the usual limitations, then you can skip them in the interests of time. If people are curious, they can ask about limitations during the question period.

How can you tell if you have the right level of detail? The best way is to practice your talk and time yourself. If you consistently go over 12 minutes, or if you have to rush, then you have too much detail. It is, we fear, as simple as that. If your talk is too long, the easiest place to chop is the Discussion. You'll rarely need more than two slides, if that many, to wrap up a brief talk. If your talk is still too long, then you need to call in reinforcements. A trusted colleague, officemate, or wallaby assistant can delete material on your behalf.

How to Avert Common Disasters

Scout the Room and Show Up Early

The wise presenter scouts the room beforehand. Will you be on a stage, behind a podium, or simply standing and talking? Is there a microphone? How big is the room? Is the projector older than you? Checking out the room will reduce your anxiety. You'll see that it's merely a room stuffed with uncomfortable stacking chairs, not a torture chamber. You will also know where the room is. At some conferences, you need a Sherpa to find your room. We have attended meetings where the talks were held in massive convention centers, in four hotels spread across three city blocks, and in a maze of dark basement rooms where even koalas fear to tread.

The mere act of showing up 15 minutes early for your talk will avert most public-speaking disasters. You'll need a few minutes to load your file onto the computer, skip through the slides to see how they look, adjust your ascot, and stash your emergency wallaby (see Chapter 4). If you need to, you can use the extra time for relaxation exercises (see Chapter 5); if not, you can chat with the moderator and other speakers.

Protect Your Slides

Save your slides in several places. Load your PowerPoint file onto a USB flash drive; as a backup, attach your file to an e-mail. To be extra cautious, you can load your file onto a friend's flash drive or bring more than one drive. This sounds excessive, but we have both lost flash drives or had drives fail. Some conferences provide computers; other conferences expect presenters to bring a computer. If each speaker expects someone else to bring a computer, then no one will have one—if you own a laptop, you might want to bring it.

Don't Talk Too Long

We've said it before, and we will say it again: Don't talk too long. A session of talks goes off the rails when one speaker takes too much time. If the first speaker goes over time, then the remaining talks must be trimmed on the fly. If several speakers go over, the last talk may be killed off. To keep the session on track, vigilant moderators will shut you down, and you will look foolish.

Paul's Woeful Tale of Woe

I'll confess that I have occasionally taken too much time during a research talk. I'm not proud of it. (In my defense, I was young and I needed the money.) At one of my first talks, the moderator began making slashing motions across her throat—that was a signal, I suspect, for me to shut the hell up and sit down. Once I learned what I was doing, however, I committed to never do this again. Taking another speaker's time is disrespectful: People travel a long way to give their talks, and they deserve their time.

As an audience member, I have seen many woeful talks in which people went disastrously over time. A few minutes over is bad but understandable—we can chalk it up to a lack of rehearsal. But why do people go over by 40 minutes?

A few years ago, I took part in a session of three talks at a small regional conference. The three speakers each had 20 minutes, and the session moderator then had 15 minutes to discuss the talks and solicit questions. I started off the session and ended under time. The next speaker, a seasoned veteran, gave a crisp, well-timed talk. But the final speaker, someone fresh out of grad school, went on and on. Discreet signals had no effect, so the moderator stood up and waited off to the side. This didn't work either, so he

(continued)

eventually interrupted the speaker—if ever a falsetto "awkward!" was deserved, it was deserved here. When the embarrassed speaker pressed the Esc key to end the slideshow, the audience could see that he was only halfway through his slides—the guy had an hour's worth of material. No time remained for a discussion or for questions, so people simply left.

At a Midwestern Psychological Association talk, I saw a speaker take 30 minutes for a 15-minute talk. To appease the moderator, he would say, "And just one more thing," until the one thing became a dozen things. Fed up, the moderator stood up midslide, nudged the speaker aside, and turned off the projector. You should fear the wrath of impatient moderators: It's easier to strangle someone when you have found the end of your rope.

The annual meeting of the Psychonomic Society has a big clock, and the attendees set their watches to this clock, known as "Psychonomic Time." (We're not making this up.) People can thus drift from room to room mid-session, knowing they won't interrupt a speaker. This could happen only in cognitive psychology—to a cognitive psychologist, 200 milliseconds is a really long time—but the idea is sound. Psychonomic Time keeps people on track. If you talk too long, you'll be gruffly cut off, and there's no gruff like cognitive-psychology gruff.

How the Session Operates

If your first talk is also your first time at a conference, here's what the session of talks will look like. Around 15 minutes before the session, the speakers drift in, coffee cups and emergency wallabies in hand, and set up their slides. After checking their slides, they usually kill the awkward pretalk nerves by chatting and milling around. You should chat with the other speakers: They study the same thing you study, so you probably have a lot in common. The audience wanders in later and, of course, prefers the back row. It's common for people to drop in late. It's annoying and distracting, but that's hypocrisy for you: We're sure that many of the latecomers excoriate their undergrads for slinking into class late.

The moderator introduces the session briefly—often as briefly as "Thanks for coming; here's our first talk"— and then the talks begin. Each person presents in the order listed in the conference program, and the moderator keeps things on track by flashing subtle signs about how much time is left. If there's time, the audience asks one or two questions after each presentation; if not, then the questions are held until the session's end. When all the talks are finished, some audience members come up to the front to chat, say hi, or ask questions that they didn't want to ask in front of everyone. And then everyone leaves, seeking restrooms and coffee, and the presenters for the next session wander in with their coffee and wallabies.

Giving Long Talks

Eventually, you'll be asked to give longer talks. If you're on an academic career path, your first longer research talk will probably be a job talk (see Chapter 9). With luck, you'll also be invited to give hour-long talks at conferences and at other universities. Giving a long talk is much like giving a short talk—you'll just be talking longer. You'll have room to stretch, to address every fascinating detail about the role of linguistic pro-forms in the disambiguation of parataxis. If you're facing your first long talk, don't worry: The mechanics are the same. Focus on what you did and found, mind the time limit, and leave the small stuff for your articles.

PONDEROUS REFLECTIONS AND CONCLUSIONS

You'll give a lot of brief research talks during your career. If you keep your talk short and focus on the major ideas, everything will go well. Then you can get to work on the one thing more painful than giving a talk about your research—writing an article about it.

8

Poster Presentations

It's a familiar scene: Graduate-student presenters stand proudly in front of their posters as an exhibit hall buzzes with onlookers. In the midst of this student hustle and bustle, you'll routinely find Dave and Paul. As experienced professionals, we probably were supposed to graduate to the "big time" and leave posters behind long ago. But we just can't do it; they're too much fun.

Poster presentations offer a number of advantages. First, they're low pressure. If you're nervous about presenting in front of a large crowd, posters are a great way to get your feet wet. Even if you royally foul up when talking about your research, only one or two people will hear it. Second, they're interactive. Posters give you a chance to converse with your audience and learn something of real value. For instance, someone may tell you about research you'd never encountered, expose you to a methodology you didn't know, or help you to hatch an evil plot for world domination. Third, posters are a great way to network. If you're a college student considering graduate school, many people who stop by your poster will be graduate students and faculty. If you're searching for a job or postdoctoral position, someone in your audience may be able to help. If you're a researcher, you could meet future collaborators.

Like most of psychology's presentation genres, posters are based on the same basic principles as any research talk. Unlike most talks, however, posters have a physical presence of paper, and possibly photographs, finger paintings, and rainbow glitter. In addition, the presenting process is somewhat different. In this chapter we'll teach you how to construct a winning poster and discuss what's unique about presenting in front of a big paper sign. Before reading further, make sure you've read Chapter 7 ("Research Talks"); most of our advice about posters builds on what we wrote there.

CREATING A POSTER

The process of creating a poster begins with an abstract. The deadline for abstract submissions is generally 6 months before the conference. Because Chapter 7 covers tips for submitting abstracts for oral presentations, we won't repeat them here. The good news is that poster abstracts are more likely to be accepted than abstracts for oral presentations. Still, the process can be competitive, so if your first attempt isn't successful, keep trying.

Once the abstract has been accepted, you'll begin constructing the poster. Think of the poster as a mini journal article, containing all the same elements—Introduction, Method (including Participants, Measures, and Procedure), Results, and Discussion. If you've already written a manuscript based on the research you'll be presenting, you'll need to reduce its size dramatically. Even more than writing a research talk, this tricky process requires a willingness to sacrifice detail for brevity. For instance, in your Measures section, you may choose to eliminate sample items and psychometric properties, leaving only a simple one-sentence description of each instrument. This is difficult for people who get too attached to every little detail of their work. For this reason, sometimes it's easier to start from scratch than to edit down a larger paper.

Most posters are created using PowerPoint. It may sound odd to use slideshow software to create a poster (and it is). Although desktop publishing software would undoubtedly allow much more creative control, PowerPoint has two distinct advantages. First, it's probably already on your computer, so you don't have to spend an arm and a leg to buy it. We know academic psychologists are wealthy, but they're often saving their money for the farmer's market or the next National Public Radio pledge drive. Second, the copy center where you'll be printing the poster also probably has it on their computer. So if you plan to use a different software package, we suggest calling the copy center first so they can tell you they've never heard of it.

Before designing your poster, find out how large it should be. Usually this information can be found in the

"Instructions to Presenters" section of the conference website. Shockingly often, however, you won't be able to find it anywhere, so don't hesitate to contact the conference organizers and ask. Although dimensions vary, probably the most common size is 36 inches × 48 inches. In PowerPoint, simply create a slide show containing one big slide with these dimensions. When you're finished, copy the file onto a CD-ROM or USB stick and bring it to the copy center. Most copy centers can print large signs in black and white. Fewer have color printing capabilities.

Large-format printing can be pricey, so if you work in a university, hospital, or research facility, check to see if they offer free poster-making services. They may even be willing to design the poster for you if you send the text. When we checked, our local copy center charged $9.00 (75 cents a square foot) to print a 36-inch × 48-inch black-and-white poster and $93.00 ($7.75 a square foot) to print it in color. Although most people use color, black and white will communicate your message just as effectively without breaking the bank.

Once you've determined the size of your poster, it's time to start writing. How much text you can fit will be determined by the size of the poster and the font. When conference attendees are surveyed, they show a distinct preference for easily readable, visually appealing posters (Waehler & Welch, 1995; Welch & Waehler, 1996). Unless you want readers to stand so close to the poster they could lick it—in which case we advise using grape scratch-and-sniff marker instead of black ink—use a font no smaller than 30 points. Font style probably doesn't matter much, though most presenters will use Times New Roman, Arial, or Helvetica.

In our experience, you can fit about 1,500 words on an average poster created with PowerPoint. This word count includes references and allows room for a couple of figures or tables. Don't think of 1,500 words as a goal, however. It's probably better to use fewer words as long as they accurately convey your work. Shorter length allows more flexibility with design and appears less confusing to readers. People can't always tell if they should read top to bottom or left to right. Extra white space and clear, bold section titles will make the poster more comprehensible. Less text also allows more room for tables, figures, and diagrams. Posters are boring without these. As detailed in Chapter 3, visuals also convey data more effectively than text alone. See Figure 8.1 for an example of a well-organized poster.

Many presenters choose not to include an abstract. Posters are kind of like long abstracts already. The advantage of including an abstract is that people casually passing by the poster can quickly get an idea of its content. The disadvantage is that it may take up nearly a fifth of your poster. Besides, an abstract might already appear in the conference program. Our recommendation is to scrap the abstract and use the extra space for tables, figures, or other visuals.

As an alternative to PowerPoint, you can use the old-fashioned method of poster construction. Only a few years back, most posters consisted of around ten

FIGURE 8.1. Example of a poster made with PowerPoint.

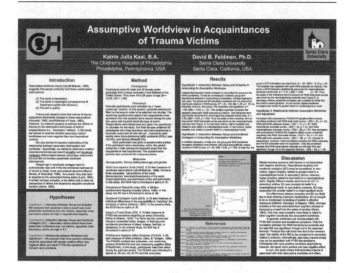

8.5-inch × 11-inch white sheets of paper mounted on slightly larger sheets of colored construction paper. Titles were either printed out one word at a time and stuck together to make a banner or simply printed on a standard-size sheet. See Figure 8.2 for an example.

This old-school method has two major advantages. First, it costs less than printing a large-format poster. This can be appealing for poor students. Second, it's much easier to transport than a large poster, which must be carried in a long poster tube. If you don't want the hassle of bag-checking your tube on the airplane, a few standard size sheets easily stack up in your carry-on luggage. In fact, there may be a resurgence of this method

106

FIGURE 8.2. Example of an old-style poster.

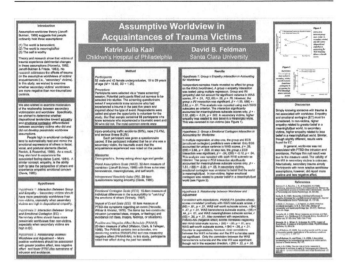

of poster construction in the works. Paul was amazed to see more old-fashioned posters at a recent conference than he had seen in several previous years combined, possibly because of the serious cash that some airlines now charge to check baggage. There are three big disadvantages of this method, however. First, the old-fashioned method fits less text. On 10 to 12 sheets of paper, you'll be limited to about 1,000 to 1,200 words. Second, your poster will look distinctly low-tech compared with many others. And third, these small sheets are substantially easier for stowaway koalas to eat. For these reasons, we generally recommend the added hassle and expense of printing a large-format poster.

POSTER CODE OF CONDUCT

Probably more important than the design of the poster is how you conduct yourself in front of it. We began this chapter by listing the many advantages of poster presentations. Notice that all of them are interpersonal in nature. How much benefit you reap from your poster in terms of learning, career networking, and collaborative contacts will depend on how you behave toward your audience. Here are some tips for maximizing the effectiveness of your poster presentation.

Engage Your Audience

Research shows that conference attendees prefer presenters who engage them in dialogue when they approach a poster (Waehler & Welch, 1995; Welch & Waehler, 1996). Unfortunately, too many presenters stand in front of their posters silently, avoiding the gaze of passers-by. Others don't even stand in front of their posters at all (see Dave's Woeful Tale of Woe). Perhaps presenters falsely believe that conversation would distract readers; maybe they fear saying something stupid. Either way, the truth is that your audience will like it if you talk to them. It is interesting that the research doesn't show any strong audience preferences about *how* presenters engage them. This takes the pressure off a bit.

Another way of avoiding engaging your audience involves talking with friends in front of your poster. We too are guilty of this common, tempting mistake. There are all kinds of reasons to do it—we haven't seen our

The first conference I ever attended was the Midwestern Psychological Association (MPA) conference in Chicago. Coming from small-town Kansas, I was excited to be in a big city and attend what felt like a huge conference. One of the greatest things about MPA was its large poster sessions. Like most regional conferences, it's a great place for graduate and even undergraduate students to try their hand at giving a first poster. I was no exception to this rule. Poster in hand, I headed from my youth hostel to the fancy conference hotel, found the exhibit hall, and pinned up my poster. Proud of myself, I began milling around, reading other posters.

Within a few minutes, however, I found myself feeling annoyed. I spotted an interesting poster, perused the text, and wanted to ask some questions. The only problem: The presenter wasn't at her poster. So, I moved on to the next poster only to have this scenario repeated. In fact, as I glanced around the room, almost half of the posters didn't have anyone standing in front of them. "How rude," I thought.

Then I realized the folly of my ways. I wasn't in front of my poster either. Everyone had done what I did, so nobody was talking to anybody. I headed back to my poster and, within minutes, was engaged in an interesting conversation with a passer-by. I'm not saying that you don't have a right to read other posters—you most certainly do. But I recommend waiting until the initial rush has subsided to do so. Just know what you're missing if you abandon your poster for long.

---

friends from other parts of the country in ages, they came by specifically to talk with us, and yakking about old times is more fun than making professional conversation with strangers. In our experience, however, interested passers-by will avoid stopping at your poster because they don't want to interrupt. If friends stop by, politely get their cell numbers and offer to get together with them later. Poster sessions only last an hour or two; you'll have the rest of the conference to spend time with them.

One of the least awkward ways of engaging your audience is to walk them through the poster. In other words, offer to give them a 3-minute spiel about your poster. This ensures that they accurately understand your research and sets the stage for productive dialogue and questions. Later in the chapter, we'll cover some tips for doing this.

Answer Questions Openly and Nondefensively

Presenting a poster gives you an opportunity to learn something about research, including how to improve your work. Unfortunately, many presenters dread this opportunity. What if someone finds something wrong with your research design? What if they ask challenging questions? What if you don't know the answers? We say, "Fantastic!" Try to view difficult questions as an opportunity to learn something. If people ask questions you don't understand, ask for clarification. If you don't know the answer, just admit it. In the extremely rare circumstance that someone is rude or aggressive in criticizing your research, try not to argue. Simply thank them for their comments and move on. Civil people behave civilly, so if someone is acting rude, it probably has more to do with them than with your poster. Far more common is the overly friendly audience member. Dave twice has had people hug him vigorously after discussing his poster. If this happens, simply disinfect with soap and water back at the hotel. For more tips on answering questions, make sure you've read Chapter 4.

Have Handouts and Other Materials Available.

After reading and discussing your poster, many people will ask for a copy. After several mishaps, Dave and Paul have determined that what they really want is a miniature copy, not the full-size version. If you used PowerPoint to design your poster, you can simply print copies on regular 8.5-inch × 11-inch paper. Alternatively, you can copy the text of the poster into a word processor document and print it out. Many presenters ask conference attendees to write down their names and promise to send them a copy via e-mail or ground mail. In an entertaining and somewhat disturbing study, however, Rienzi and Allen (1994) found that only 51% of presenters at three major psychology conferences made good on this promise. Dave suspects he was in the sample. So that you're not featured in their next study, we suggest bringing 30 copies of your poster with you. You might also want to have other materials available. For instance, we always bring at least one copy of the surveys and stimulus materials used in the research. This may be useful if someone asks specific questions about methodology.

THE 3-MINUTE SPIEL

As mentioned in the previous section, you should prepare a 3- to 5-minute summary of your poster, practice it, and be ready to deliver it several times during the session. It's not easy to condense complex research into a brief spiel, so this will take serious thought. Whatever you do, don't just read your poster; this takes way too much time, and conference attendees can do it on their own. The job of your spiel is to stimulate conversation, not exhaustively summarize your study. Remember, the advantages of presenting a poster are interpersonal; saying too much in your spiel will foreclose on the opportunity for further discussion. Here's a suggested outline for your spiel with rough time estimates:

- Introduction (30 seconds–1 minute): Begin with two or three sentences conveying why you chose to do the study. Avoid the temptation to launch into a detailed literature review. If audience members want more background on the research area, they'll ask for it.
- Method (1–2 minutes): Prepare a couple of paragraphs about your participants, measures, and procedure. This should be a very general summary. As an example, here are the Participants and Procedure sections from a poster, followed by the spiel version of the same sections.

Participants

Participants were 52 male and 43 female undergraduates from a large university in the Midwest of the

United States. They were 18 to 29 years of age (M = 18.82, SD = 1.25).

Procedure

Potential participants were selected via a "mass screening" session. In this session, potential participants filled out surveys in order to be selected into studies. The screening questionnaire asked if the respondents knew someone who had experienced a trauma during the past 5 years and inquired about the type of event. Respondents were telephoned and given the opportunity to volunteer for the study. Our final sample contained 65 participants who knew someone who had experienced a traumatic event and 30 who did not. Among the most commonly cited events were injury-producing traffic accidents (60%), rape (15.4%), and serious illness (6.2%).

Each participant was given a questionnaire packet. If the participant had indicated that he or she was a secondary victim, the packet contained a note naming the traumatic event that the acquaintance had experienced. The questionnaire packets also contained the measures below.

And here's the spiel version:

Potential participants were prescreened and selected from a much larger "mass testing" sample. Sixty-five college students who said they knew someone who had experienced a trauma and 30 who didn't filled out our final questionnaire packets. You can see here [point to the poster] that participants' acquaintances had experienced a wide variety of traumatic events. Let me briefly tell you about the measures we used . . .

■ Results and Discussion (1–2 minutes): Write another couple of paragraphs summarizing the results and implications of your study. To reduce time, we suggest combining the Results and Discussion sections in your spiel, whether or not they're combined on your poster.

After you've developed the spiel, practice it several times until you've committed it to memory. You don't have to memorize it word for word, but know it well enough to no longer need notes. Time yourself. If you're consistently taking more than 3 to 5 minutes, eliminate a few sentences and try again. Sometimes this process takes several hours. Trust us, you and your audience will be happy you made the effort.

PONDEROUS REFLECTIONS AND CONCLUSIONS

Many people think that posters aren't presentations. The truth is that posters are every bit as much about presenting as research talks. Don't miss this great opportunity to chat with people who are actually interested in your work. Whether you're hoping to solicit critiques and advice about your work, meet potential research collaborators, or devise a scheme for global domination, you may meet that special helpful someone standing right in front of your poster.

9

Job Talks

Throughout this book, we've attempted to calm your fears. People often anticipate that horrific dinosaur-killing catastrophes will befall their presentations, only to discover that things normally go pretty well. In our experience, however, it's frequently the opposite with job talks—people don't fear them enough. Here's why: By the time you work your way up to a job talk, you've probably given at least one other presentation. Maybe you've presented a poster, talked at a conference or two, or even taught a course. Now you know what you're doing, right?

Wrong! Wrong, wrong, wrong, wrong, wrong. (Wrong.) We're not saying you should be afraid. As discussed in Chapter 5, fear is only a wise strategy when presenting to man-eating grizzly bears, which is unlikely given the odd lack of human faculty at man-eating grizzly bear universities. But the result of people's low anxiety about job talks can be an alarming dearth of preparation. We've seen many seasoned speakers royally screw up. For instance, when a well-published, nationally known scholar applied for a job at Paul's university, many of the faculty were excited to put a face and personality to the excellent research they had read. What they got was 45 minutes of the most exquisitely boring, fastidiously detailed note-reading behavior ever witnessed.

Our bet is that this preeminent psychologist probably thought, "A job talk is no big deal, it's just another research presentation." To his credit, he accurately and thoroughly communicated his research. This kind of talk would have been fine at many conferences—a little boring, but fine. At conferences, people genuinely are there to learn about your research. Not true of job talks. Although job talks officially are about research, they're actually about something more fundamental. Knowing what they're really about will give you an enormous advantage over the unenlightened masses who you're going to ruthlessly beat out of a job. Your competition may be talented, freakishly intelligent, and accomplished, but you know the rules of the game. That's how Dave consistently beats his cat at chess.

In this chapter, we'll cover two important principles for honing and focusing your talk. Then, we'll discuss the nuts and bolts of developing and delivering a great research-oriented job talk. Before we begin, we should say a word about two types of job talks. Virtually all colleges and universities will ask you to give a research-oriented presentation. A much smaller number may ask you to teach a sample class. Because of the sheer variety of topics on which you might be asked to speak, it's almost impossible to specify the elements of this latter type of presentation, so we'll primarily concentrate on research job talks in this chapter. That doesn't mean that this chapter won't be useful if you're not giving a research talk. If you've been asked to give a sample lecture, you've probably taught classes before. Our advice is to do what you'd normally do, paying special attention to the two principles we're about to discuss.

TWO PRINCIPLES FOR FOCUSING YOUR JOB TALK

Principle #1: Job Talks Aren't Actually about Research

Job talks are really about you. Research is just a convenient excuse to convey who you are and what you'll bring to the institution. The committee already knows a ton about you: They've seen your vita, read your teaching and research statements, talked to some of your recommenders. They even may even have read some of your published work. They know you're qualified.

What they don't know is if you're nice. Yes, they actually care about this. Faculty jobs are hard to come by. If it's a tenure-track position, you're likely to stay for a long time—maybe even for the rest of your career. They're trying to find out if you're the kind of person they want to invite into their lives and fight over office space with for the next 20 years. So, don't hide yourself. Don't be afraid to be funny or expressive, if that's who you are. Don't be afraid to convey your passion to the audience or share a story about yourself.

As with all other talks, the audience is on your side. They asked you to speak because they like you. Out of numerous applicants, they chose you to be among the three or four people they'll interview. They're hoping that every candidate they've invited is excellent. The greater each of you is, the better choice they'll have. Many of the people in your audience already will have a warm fuzzy feeling just thinking about you. Remembering this may help you relax and let your fabulous little self shine though.

Of course, if you're the type of person who tends to appear stuck up or conceited—though you would probably have no idea if that actually was you—don't go overboard. Give some serious thought to how you're going to convey the wonderful things about you without looking like a jackass. Considering the following questions may help:

- How did you develop your research interests? Sometimes there's an intriguing or entertaining personal story behind your work. As long as it's relatively short (2 or 3 minutes) and socially appropriate, consider sharing it. We strongly recommend keeping long stories about childhood trauma under your belt for now. They may be meaningful and relevant, but they also might make you look crazy or desperate.

- How will you involve students in research? Your work presents opportunities for students, or at least it should. Students learn through hands-on experience; your future faculty wants to know how you'll help provide this.

- What special skills or interests will you bring to the department? If your research or teaching adds something compelling to the department, make sure to highlight this. For instance, if you are a stats guru, consider tastefully mentioning how much you look forward to being of help to fellow faculty. Your mad ping-pong skills should probably be left for discussion in one-on-one interviews.

- What are your aspirations for future research or teaching? How you answer this question will be of particular interest to your future colleagues. This may be the best predictor of what you'll do on arriving at the school.

It can be challenging to address these issues while simultaneously conveying the merit and sophistication of your research. Despite our comments to the contrary, job talks aren't actually personal ads. You can't let the research pretense drop. Later in the chapter, we'll address concretely how to strike this delicate balance.

Principle #2: Know your Audience and What They Expect

We realize that we already discussed it in Chapter 2. Nonetheless, knowing your audience is even more important in job talks than other presentations. At most colleges and universities, the audience is composed primarily of faculty members. But, who are these people?

Are they all from your department or profession? Are they predominantly researchers, teachers, or a mixture? Do they have any prior knowledge of your particular research area? Are there any administrators present? Many schools also invite students to these talks. If there will be students present, will they be undergraduates? Doctoral students? Masters students? How long have they been at the university? What are their interests? Will they be allowed to bring pets?

Knowledge of your audience is important because it allows you to tailor both the level and content of your talk. If undergrads will be attending, it's a good idea to include at least one fart joke. (We're kidding—undergrads are much more interested in sex.) Within the confines of good taste and relevance, however, it's wise to judiciously make reference to subjects your audience cares about.

You may wonder what to do if the audience is a mixture of people. Maybe you've got undergraduates held captive in the back of the room, faculty in the front, and a few graduate students scattered throughout. A couple of approaches may work here. First, you could pitch your talk somewhere in the middle. Be warned: This is a really hard thing to do. The danger is that the undergraduates will think you're a stuck-up intellectual with nothing practical to say, and faculty will think you're a pop-psych nitwit. For this reason, we suggest using this option with caution. If you ultimately choose to split the difference, here's our suggestion—

don't dumb down the whole talk. Instead, deliver the talk at a sophisticated level, then pause occasionally to summarize in plain English what you've said. At some point, also spend a minute or two addressing the real-life relevance of your work. This will satisfy both the faculty's need for sophistication and the undergraduates' need to understand what you're talking about.

A second approach to mixed audiences may be somewhat easier to pull off. This strategy involves first figuring out who the most important people in your audience are, then addressing your talk primarily to them. For instance, if you're interviewing at a college that is primarily dedicated to undergraduate education, and the undergrads will be providing feedback about you, then consider pitching your talk directly to them. On the other hand, if the school is very PhD-centric and the faculty couldn't care less about their auditorium-style undergraduate courses, then consider pitching your talk almost exclusively to faculty and graduate students.

How do you find out who will be in your audience and what they expect from you? Ask. When you're invited for an interview, be sure to ask a few simple questions: Whom will I be speaking to? How long should the talk be? How much time should I leave for questions? Is there anything specific I should address in the talk? Asking these questions may seem a bit awkward at the time you're offered the interview, but it will be a lot less awkward than misgauging your talk later on.

The basic elements of a job talk are similar to a standard research talk. First, you'll give an introduction, followed by the methods and results of a study or two. You'll end by discussing the implications of these results, predicting future directions for investigation, and offering a brief conclusion. For more details about the specific elements of research talks, take a look at Chapter 7. There are a few differences between job talks and standard research presentations, however. Superficially, job talks are a lot longer. Conference research presentations typically last about 15 minutes, whereas job talks generally last an hour or more with questions. Additionally, there are two more fundamental differences between job talks and research presentations, both of which flow from the principles just discussed.

First, throughout the talk, you'll want to emphasize how you match what the faculty is looking for. Be familiar with the job posting, and show how you meet its requirements. When Dave applied for his current job, the posting called for a clinical psychologist specializing in cognitive–behavior therapy (CBT). Dave certainly had a background in CBT, but he didn't exactly "specialize" in it. Actually, he was much more integrationist in therapy style. But this was not the time to let his open-minded eclecticism shine through. Throughout his presentation, he subtly used terms like *cognition*, *self-talk*, and *reinforcement contingencies* to describe aspects of his research on hope and life meaning. Although he might just as easily have borrowed language from existential–humanistic thought, it was important to communicate that he was versed in the language and constructs of CBT. The ruse worked. Now, he's happily subverting students to an integrationist approach to psychotherapy everyday. Of course, don't lie. Dave really is an expert in CBT; he just chooses to integrate other perspectives as well. If you really don't match the job posting, don't try to stretch or contort to fit. The faculty will see through your disguise. Just be yourself. After all, they invited you there for a reason.

Second, the conclusion of job talks should be somewhat different than other research presentations. In most hour-long research talks, you can acknowledge shortcomings of your studies and suggest future directions for investigation. This also is true of job talks, with one important caveat: You're not speaking to a generic audience. Because you're talking to possible future colleagues, you've got the opportunity to customize things a bit. Instead of addressing future directions for research *in general*, discuss directions for research *at this institution*. Here are some issues you might choose to comment on: (a) research you would like to do in the future, (b) how this research would involve students, (c) faculty with whom you might naturally enjoy collaborations, (d) any grants for which you plan to apply, and (e) any local organizations you would like to involve (e.g., nonprofits, hospitals, clinics, churches). Don't worry if you don't have enough information to address all of these points. Just cover what seems most relevant. Familiarizing yourself with the school by reading its website and any other literature you can get your hands on will help immensely with this part of the talk. They'll be impressed that you've given thought to how your work fits with the institution.

DELIVERING THE TALK
AND ANSWERING QUESTIONS

If you've prepared well, delivering the presentation should seem like a natural next step. You've determined who's in your audience, what your time limit is, what research you're going to cover, and what you're going to say about yourself. Now, have fun with your talk. As we said up front, out of a large pool of applicants, a group of scholars has asked you to speak on a topic that you care about. Allow yourself to feel honored. Most likely, things will go as planned and you'll give a great talk. But what if something unanticipated happens? What if something goes wrong?

As we discussed in Chapter 6, mishaps during speaking engagements are relatively rare. Nonetheless, you may fear that in their continued plot to undermine academia and replace university campuses with eucalyptus plantations, koalas will sabotage your job talk. With their wily little fingers, they may tear light bulbs from computer projectors, steal laptop power adapters, and even take down campuswide wireless networks (see

Chapter 3 for more information about the infamous World Wide Koalavirus).

But such technology malfunctions are no match for you. You're prepared with backups. Along with the primary copy of your PowerPoint slides (probably on a USB stick), we would recommend having several backup copies on other media—CD, in your e-mail inbox, another USB stick, another CD, another e-mail inbox. If these fail, which they sometime do, fear not: You've gone old-school and brought along a set of overhead transparencies. Yes, we know we said in Chapter 6 that overheads are overrated. No, we're not hypocrites. Most of the time you're going to give talks in hotels and conference centers. They generally don't have overhead projectors available. Universities usually still do. So, bring transparencies, just in case. Of course, if all else fails, you always can go low-tech and have the audience refer to handouts.

Probably the part of the job talk that novices fear most is the question-and-answer session. People sometimes are so afraid of answering questions that their talk conveniently invades Q&A time, cutting it in half or worse. It is essential that you not let this happen. This portion of the presentation is your chance to speak informally with the faculty, showing them that you're intelligent, thoughtful, and willing to listen to constructive criticism. Many of the faculty won't be able to interview you individually, so the Q&A session may be the only time they can interact with you. Just be yourself and answer questions in a thoughtful, balanced way. If someone asks a question you don't understand, ask him or her to rephrase it. If you need further clarification, politely ask for it.

Although there's always the chance that people will attack, there's no incentive for doing this. It just makes them look like jerks. After all, they're the ones who invited you to speak, usually paying for your travel, room, and board. Still, it can happen. If someone attacks, this simple four-step procedure will protect you from most harm:

- First, check the integrity of your 20-gauge protective chain mail. This usually guards against any biting or shoes launched across the room.

- Second, don't get defensive. Do your best to avoid arguing or defending yourself at all. The old adage is true—it takes two to tango but only one to break-dance. Your job is to break-dance. You don't need to dance with the mean person; you can do your own sexy dance.

- Third, compliment the big meany. If you can stomach it, comment on how much worth you see in the criticisms. Sometimes this involves searching for the small grain of truth in what he or she has said and acknowledging its value. Mention that if you wind up working at the school, you'll look forward to collaborating to address his or her concerns. If your spine isn't quite that flexible, simply paraphrase the critique and thank the person for the insightful comment. Then move on. Much of the time, your attacker just needs his or her ego stroked.

- Fourth, if you're comfortable, speak with the attacking person about it after the talk. Act really interested. You may just turn an adversary into an advocate.

For an example of this procedure in action, see Dave's Woeful Tale of Woe.

Dave's Woeful Tale of Woe

My first job interview was at a small Midwestern college. The job talk was to take place in the early evening, after a long string of faculty interviews. I have to confess, things were going pretty well. It seemed strange, however, that several faculty went out of their way to make sure I was prepared for the talk. "You ready for your talk later this evening?" they asked. Shaking my hand good-bye and smiling, one of them even assured me, "Don't worry if anything goes wrong."

"Smile and nod," I told myself.

The talk detailed my research on the mental and physical benefits of hopeful cognition, focusing on a randomized control trial demonstrating that hope could be raised in a sample of community-dwelling adults. It seemed to go relatively well, except for the fact that a middle-aged gentleman smack in the middle of the room kept breathing deeply and rolling his eyes. Then came the dreaded question-and-answer portion. The first two questions were no sweat. Then eye-rolling man raised his hand. "Don't you think hope is just a stupid concept?" he asked. "Why don't you talk about something that really matters? All you're really talking about is self-confidence anyhow."

(continued)

Smile and nod.

Even intelligent people can be jerks. Luckily, my faculty mentor had prepared me for just such comments. "Don't get into a fight," he said. "Just find the grain of truth in what they say, acknowledge it, and move on." So, that's what I did. Looking the fellow right in the eyes, I smiled and said, "You've got a really really good point; many people believe that concepts like hope are really just proxies for self-confidence or self-efficacy. I'm comfortable calling hope by any of these other names, if you'd like. I really appreciate your comment." Believe it or not, it actually worked. After a couple of similar volleys, he backed down, pleased that he had kicked my intellectual butt.

Afterwards, three faculty members congratulated me on handling the mean guy's question well. A week later, I was offered the job. The chair of the search committee even commented that she was impressed by how well I kept my cool. "Most people end up getting into an argument with him," she said. It was an important lesson for me: The faculty knew he was a big jerk and were embarrassed about it. They were on my side. I'm happy to report, however, that I took a job at another school where I wasn't attacked during my talk.

PONDEROUS REFLECTIONS AND CONCLUSIONS

Congratulations, you've finished your job talk. (Yes, we realize that you're reading this before giving your talk. Just play along.) You're probably away from home in a place you've never been before. Go out and explore the town, eat at a good restaurant, or order room service. The next day, write a brief thank-you e-mail to the chair of the search committee and whoever else invited you to speak. It doesn't have to say anything fancy, just a few sentences expressing how much you enjoyed visiting with the faculty and appreciate them inviting you. If you continue to be interested in the job, be sure to express this enthusiasm as well. You'll hear back from them within a few weeks. If they offer you the job, congratulations! If they don't, you've joined the ranks of most academics and both of the authors of this book.

10

Presentations for Lay Audiences

We psychologists are bad at publicizing our work. Unless you're a clinical or counseling psychologist, for instance, you probably have no idea that certain kinds of psychotherapy beat medication for treating some anxiety disorders and basically tie medication for treating depression, though with lower relapse rates (Butler, Chapman, Forman, & Beck, 2006). That's pretty cool stuff, right? Then why does the general public still think drugs rule?

Part of it has to do with money—drug companies are rich and powerful. A lot of it, however, stems from the fact that medical professionals are better than us at talking to the lay public. In our training, psychologists are discouraged from communicating with laypeople. We're told that colleagues who write and speak for general audiences are "lightweight." Those who attempt to publicize the field's knowledge are branded with the derogatory labels of "pop-psychologist" or "self-help guru."

Many academics wrongly belittle speaking to lay audiences because they're not very good at it. It's easier to condemn this difficult skill than to learn it. And it doesn't come naturally for most of us. Dave once tried to explain his research on the relationship between goal-directed cognition and life meaning to his grandfather. He delivered a stunning lecture peppered with such heart-pounding terms as *attribution theory*, *locus of control*, and *pathways thinking*, even managing to work in some statistics. After listening attentively for 5 minutes, his grandfather correctly responded, "That's egghead stuff. What's for dinner?" There are some valuable lessons in this experience: Laypeople aren't impressed by psychobabble, they aren't captivated by our anal-retentive scientific methodologies, they don't even care about our brilliant theories. They're not stupid, either. Dave's grandpa was a doctor!

The trick to presenting to laypeople isn't to dumb things down but to determine how your work addresses issues of significance to your audience. In this chapter, we'll cover how to tune your message to achieve this goal, allowing you to reach beyond your narrow field of study to influence the larger world.

DECIDING WHAT TO TALK ABOUT

The first step in constructing a talk for the lay public is deciding what to talk about. Because it's not your usual audience, this can be tricky. We're used to speaking to others like ourselves—nerds. Nerds care about psychology for the sake of psychology; they're fascinated by theory, methodology, and data. Normal people usually aren't. Instead, they care about things that matter concretely in their everyday lives. They're prone to asking pesky questions like, "What does this have to do with the real world?"; "Am I any better off after hearing this?"; and even "So what?"

A good way to figure out what may interest the general public is to search your heart for what really matters to you, not as a psychologist, but as a human being. Think back to what excited you about entering the field. You may have been naive back then, but we'd bet your motivations were purer. Dave and Paul, for instance, began studying psychology to analyze people. Yes, we also enjoyed research and dreamed of being professors, but our true motivations were much simpler. What really floated Dave's boat was psyching people out, understanding what made them tick, and using this knowledge to help them overcome mental illness. For Paul, it was always about brainwashing people to believe that koalas were trying to take over the world. Many of us roll our eyes when undergraduates say things like, "I'm majoring in psychology because I'm always analyzing people anyways." Nonetheless, the public eats this stuff up. And, truth be told, don't we too? Maybe you went into psychology to help people, cure yourself, end prejudice, or create a super-intelligent robot to exterminate humankind. If it matters to you, chances are it matters to others.

If you truly did dream of being a psychologist to learn about the binomial effect size display, consider a

133

different method for determining what might interest a general audience. Suppose you've been invited to speak to a group of young mothers. Do a bit of research on this audience—read their magazines, watch their television shows, eavesdrop on their Internet blogs, steal a baby. You'll quickly discover that they care about stuff like whether their child is hyperactive, how their kids can do better at school, how to get the little angels to behave, and how to protect them from baby stealers.

Once you've identified a topic that you believe matters to the lay public, consider how you might use your research and professional knowledge to address this issue. Then start writing your presentation.

HOW TO AVOID BORING YOUR AUDIENCE

Of course, writing a presentation for the general public isn't as simple as it sounds. Academics are renowned for boring people to death. Because most of us have been trained to speak to nerds, it's easy to forget how to speak to regular human beings. Here are some tips to help avoid putting your audience to sleep.

Avoid Pretentious Language and Jargon

Although the employment of lavish elocution may lend an air of erudition to an otherwise pedestrian address, the utility of said terminology is appreciably curtailed by the paucity of comprehension among individuals in broad-spectrum society. Despite an academic zeitgeist compelling the utilization of aforementioned pretentious verbal behavior, those in observance likely will construe such comportment as sophistry. On the contrary, we advocate availing oneself of the vulgate, thus maximizing positive affect among addressees while concomitantly ensuring their efficient assimilation of information into extant cognitive schemata. In other words, don't be a big fat stuck-up windbag. We're not suggesting that you dumb down your talk (for ample reason to avoid this, see Dave's Woeful Tale of Woe). Just speak like a normal person and remember that your listeners neither carry an *Oxford English Dictionary* in their pockets nor speak fluent psychobabble.

Dave's Woeful Tale of Woe

Recently, I was asked to present at a local church on the topic "What Every Family Should Know About Terminal Illness." The audience primarily was composed of people over the age of 65 who were either concerned about their own health or were caring for someone with a serious disease. My presentation lasted for about a half hour, followed by another half hour of questions.

Audience members were facing difficult problems in their lives, and their questions often conveyed a sense of concern and even desperation. They listened courteously and attentively, clearly appreciative of the information being provided. Situations like this are hard for speakers, because it's necessary to answer questions in a nonjargony, easy-to-understand way without oversimplifying the complex issues in audience members' lives.

This last point is illustrated clearly by what happened to the speaker who followed me. Presenting on legal and ethical issues

(continued)

surrounding the end of life, he tended to oversimplify issues and talk down to the audience. He actually spent 5 minutes explaining what a lawyer was. The audience mauled him during the question-and-answer period. One listener even declared loudly that he disagreed and walked out of the session early.

The same audience that listened appreciatively during my talk displayed indignation during his. This wasn't attributable to his qualifications or the information he presented—both were impeccable. He just sounded a bit too much like a kindergarten teacher. Although lay audiences may not know all the terminology that you do, they're usually composed of smart people, and it's important to treat them as such.

Don't Speak in Abstractions

Abstract sentences refer indirectly to people without explicitly mentioning them. Here's an example: "The avoidance symptoms of posttraumatic stress disorder at the end of life include social isolation and communication difficulties that can interfere with access to competent medical care." Pretty boring, huh? Concrete sentences put life back into desiccated statements by including characters: "People suffering from posttraumatic stress disorder at the end of their lives often avoid others and isolate themselves; this may affect their ability to communicate well with doctors and, as a result, can hurt their medical care." The more you use statements containing people, the more your audience will sit up and listen.

Realize That Only You Care About Statistics

In the intensive brainwashing process called graduate school, our professors tried hard to make us believe that there's nothing more fascinating than research. Many of us savor clever studies, obsess over research design, and dream about data analysis. Although you may want your wedding cake decorated in an SPSS theme, most laypeople don't share your fixation. Of course, research methodology and data analysis are indispensable; without them, we couldn't know anything about the world with certainty. Unfortunately, the audience doesn't care. This doesn't mean you can't talk about research, just don't do it in a nerdy way. Instead, briefly summarize the research, emphasizing the findings (in plain language, not stat-speak) rather than geeking out on the methodological details.

Tell Stories

Another objective of our graduate-school brainwashing was to teach us that stories aren't meaningful. We label insights drawn from stories as "anecdotal" and disregard them as not generalizable. Although it's true that particular instances in isolation don't tell us much about the broader world, many stories are great illustrations of trends in the data. And stories are infinitely more attention-grabbing than statistics. According to William Kilpatrick (1983) in his book, *Psychological Seduction*, stories are more likely than rational arguments to convince people. It probably has something to do with evolution.

When Ug came back from hunting yaks and told his tribe about a group of 10 tigers beyond the ridge that stalked him for 3 hours, nobody asked whether the probability of encountering so many tigers at once was statistically significant. Instead, they avoided the ridge. We're the beneficiaries of their wise genes, so we too care about stories. To keep your audience's interest, we recommend including at least one story every 15 to 20 minutes. Such tales don't have to be long (maybe a minute or two each), but they should clearly illustrate the points you're making.

Talk About Real-World Implications

As mentioned previously, general audiences want to know how your work affects their world—the real world. Although most psychology research has immediate implications for laypeople, we're often reticent to share these implications. This reticence may in part stem from a common misinterpretation of the American Psychological Association ethics code. Specifically, section 5.01 states, "Psychologists do not knowingly make public statements that are false, deceptive, or fraudulent concerning their research, practice, or other work activities" (APA, 2002, p. 1067). Many psychologists think this means that they can't make inferences from data. At a recent conference, Dave even overheard someone say that she would never do media interviews because anything the interviewer asked would require her to "stray from the data." No offense, but that's stupid.

Research is always incomplete; that's why we do more of it. It's okay to draw reasonable conclusions from the data as long as you're using a process of logical inference. For instance, if you only have correlational data, it's probably okay to speculate about causal relationships. When doing this, keep things honest by using words like *possibly* or *probably* and phrases like, "We can't know for sure from the data, but my theory is . . . " Caveats like these allow you to discuss the real-world implications of research without abandoning scientific integrity.

Leave Your Audience with a Take-Away Message

A fantastic way of ending a talk to the lay public is to offer a take-away message that's relevant to your listeners' lives. Take-away messages summarize what you've discussed and leave your audience with something to think about on their drive home. "Research should continue to address the influence of hopeful thinking on the goal-pursuit process" isn't a good take-away message because your audience doesn't care about research. You don't have to completely change your message, however. It's possible to say something similar, but with more relevance to your listeners:

> So, hopeful thinking increases our likelihood of achieving the goals that are important to us. In coming years, our research team hopes to learn even more about how high-hope people establish successful lives, so that we can share this knowledge with others.

In contrast to the first example, this one emphasizes the effect that such research will have on real people's lives.

FINDING OPPORTUNITIES TO SPEAK

If you're planning to give a presentation to the general public, it's probably because you've been asked to do so. Most speakers don't locate these opportunities themselves; rather, they're invited by a lay organization that has heard about their work. Nonetheless, you can make your own opportunities by contacting organizations directly. Give some thought to what community organizations or venues suit your topic. Who's likely to be interested in what you have to say? Where can you find these people? What groups do they belong to? Here are some organizations and venues to consider:

- Churches and synagogues
- Schools
- Libraries
- Bookstores (especially if you've written a book)
- Adult and senior-citizen education programs
- Parenting groups
- Nonpsychology professional organizations

Many of these organizations are happy for experts like you to speak about topics that are relevant to what they do, especially if you'll do it for free. Once you've determined which venue is right, send them an e-mail asking if they would be interested in having you speak.

You can find the e-mail address of an appropriate contact person on most organizations' websites. For churches and synagogues, you'll generally write the minister or rabbi. For libraries, the head librarian is usually a good contact person. Bookstores usually have an event coordinator in charge of speaking engagements and book signings. Other organizations are more variable. If it's not obvious, simply call and inquire about the best person to contact.

In your e-mail, introduce yourself, describe your expertise, and briefly explain your proposed talk. See Exhibit 10.1 for a sample letter. Be sure to state that you

---

EXHIBIT 10.1   Sample Proposal Letter

March 1, 2008

Dear Reverend Johnson:

Greetings. I am an assistant professor of counseling psychology at Santa Clara University and coauthor of *The End-of-Life Handbook: A Compassionate Guide to Connecting With and Caring for a Dying Loved One*. My coauthor is S. Andrew Lasher Jr., MD, Director of Palliative Medicine at the California Pacific Medical Center in San Francisco. I am writing because I know that your church has a speaker series that has featured presentations on health-related topics in the past. My coauthor and I would like to volunteer to speak on the topic, "What Every Family Should Know About Life-Threatening and Terminal Illness." I believe that this subject may be of great interest to your congregation, especially those with aging parents or loved ones.

As the baby boomer generation ages, more and more people are facing the prospect of caring for parents and other loved ones with

---

(continued)

EXHIBIT 10.1. Sample Proposal Letter *(continued)*

life-threatening and terminal illnesses. With the stunning capability of modern medical technology, they have more choices than ever before about how and where the end of life will occur. Unfortunately, most people are unprepared for the responsibility of making such choices. The families of our patients frequently express a desire to understand more fully what their loved ones are going through and how best to help. Medical providers, for their part, often observe that family misunderstandings present barriers to patients getting the best care possible. A talk on this topic could inform your congregation about the importance of end-of-life issues and prepare them for the challenge of caregiving during this difficult stage of life.

We would be thrilled if you would consider inviting us to speak about "What Every Family Should Know About Life-Threatening and Terminal Illness." This topic is extremely important to us, and we consider it our mission to help families facing this difficult caregiving journey. As such, we would be happy to speak at no charge. I've attached information about us and our book to this e-mail. For additional information and clips from recent radio interviews, you can also visit our website at http://www.endoflifehandbook.com. If I can answer any questions, please do not hesitate to contact me by phone or e-mail. I look forward to hearing from you.

Sincerely,
David B. Feldman, PhD
Department of Counseling Psychology
Santa Clara University

aren't asking for money (unless you are). You might also consider saying why you're willing to give the talk for free so they know there's no catch. In other words, why is this topic important for you and your potential audience?

In our experience, your hit rate will be about 25%. Although some organizations may be thrilled to have you speak, others won't even respond. Don't get discouraged; you can't know why they're not interested. Just accept it and move on. Once you've given a talk, feel free to ask the event coordinator for a brief endorsement letter. If the letter is good, you can quote it when writing to other organizations. A simple quote, like "Paul Silvia's talk on the history of the koala uprising in North America was informative and interesting; everyone benefited enormously," will increase your attractiveness to other lay organizations.

PONDEROUS REFLECTIONS AND CONCLUSIONS

Imagine what would happen if every research-oriented psychologist delivered at least one presentation to the lay public. Maybe the world would be a better place. Maybe people would stop thinking we're quacks. Maybe we'd get paid more. Who knows? Let's find out.

Epilogue

Thanks for reading our book. Writing it was a labor of love, and we hope that it has been helpful to you. Many people told us, "Nobody will want to read your paranoid ramblings about koalas," but we persisted, overcoming all odds to get our message out. Don't be fooled by the way they placidly cuddle up against the eucalyptus tree in your local zoo; those crafty little paws may one day engineer the downfall of civilization. We don't think this is at all paranoid or "totally nuts," as some have unfairly opined. The evidence is everywhere, but we'll leave that for you to decide.

We apologize that most of this book concerned public speaking; it was the only way we could convince the publisher to print it. Although you undoubtedly read the book to learn about the great koala threat, you may also have learned a thing or two about giving our profession's most common presentations. Our guidelines are simple, yet many people fail to follow them: First, know your audience. It is on this principle that all good talks are built. Keeping this in mind will ensure the relevance of your message to those in attendance. Second, know that the audience is on your side. They're there because they want to be, and they know that presenting can be difficult. Keeping this in mind will make planning and delivering the presentation seem less daunting. Third, plan for common problems. Doing this will make sure that even if the projector stops working or someone asks a stupid question, these minor mishaps won't blossom into full-fledged disasters. Fourth, know that even the best presenters feel anxiety. Realizing this may help you to cut yourself a break, even if the presentation falls short of your expectations. Finally, always stash an emergency wallaby in the rafters. We trust that the reasons for this are self-explanatory.

Following these guidelines will enable you to give talks that both interest and educate fellow scholars as well as the lay public. They may even help you to get a job. But none of that matters if koalas take over, does it?

References

American Psychological Association. (2002). Ethical principles of psychologists and code of conduct. *American Psychologist, 57*, 1060–1073.

Anderson, C. A. (1983). Imagination and expectation: The effect of imagining behavioral scripts on personal intentions. *Journal of Personality and Social Psychology, 45*, 293–305.

Beck, A. T. (1979). *Cognitive therapy and the emotional disorders*. New York, NY: Meridian.

Beck, J. S. (1995). *Cognitive therapy: Basics and beyond*. New York, NY: Guilford Press.

Burns, D. D. (1999). *Feeling good: The new mood therapy*. New York, NY: Avon.

Butler, A. C., Chapman, J. E., Forman, E. M., & Beck, A. T. (2006). The empirical status of cognitive–behavioral therapy: A review of meta-analyses. *Clinical Psychology Review, 26*, 17–31.

Ellis, A. (1999). *Reason and emotion in psychotherapy: A comprehensive method for treating human disturbances*. New York, NY: Citadel.

Endicott, J. (1999). For the prepared presenter, fonts of inspiration abound. *Presentations, 13*, 22–23.

Feldman, D. B., & Silvia, P. J. (2008, August). *Causal effects of APA Style on modes of scholarly communication: The case of caffeine-induced interpersonal discourse*. Unpublished gossip at the 116th Annual Convention of the American Psychological Association, Boston, MA.

Felz, D. L., & Landers, D. M. (1983). The effects of mental practice on motor skills learning and performance: A meta-analysis. *Journal of Sport Psychology, 5*, 25–57.

Frankfurt, H. G. (2005). *On bullshit*. Princeton, NJ: Princeton University Press.

Fredrickson, B. L. (2000). Extracting meaning from past affective experiences: The importance of peaks, ends, and specific emotions. *Cognition and Emotion, 14*, 577–606.

Hallett, T. L., & Faria, G. (2006). Teaching with multimedia: Do bells and whistles help students learn? *Journal of Technology in Human Services, 24*, 167–179.

Jacobson, E. (1938). *Progressive relaxation*. Chicago, IL: University of Chicago Press.

Kalyuga, S., Chandler, P., & Sweller, J. (2004). When redundant on-screen text in multimedia technical instruction can interfere with learning. *Human Factors, 46*, 567–581.

Kilpatrick, W. (1983). *Psychological seduction*. New York, NY: Thomas Nelson.

Kingery, D., & Furuta, R. (1997). Skimming electronic newspaper headlines: A study of typeface, point size, screen resolution, and monitor size. *Information Processing and Management, 33*, 685–696.

Kozasa, E. H., & Leite, J. R. (1998). A brief protocol of cognitive modification and gradual exposure for reduction of fear symptoms of public speaking. *Journal of Behavior Therapy and Experimental Psychiatry, 29*, 317–326.

Larson, R. B. (2004). Slide composition for electronic presentations. *Journal of Education Computing Research, 31*, 61–76.

Leahy, W., Sweller, J., & Chandler, P. (2003). When auditory presentation should and should not be a component of multimedia instruction. *Applied Cognitive Psychology, 17,* 401–418.

LeDoux, J. (1996). *The emotional brain.* New York, NY: Simon & Schuster.

Rienzi, B. M., & Allen, M. J. (1994). Poster presenters: Send us your papers. *American Psychologist, 49,* 681–682.

Reynolds, G. (2008). *Presentation Zen: Simple ideas on presentation design and delivery.* Berkeley, CA: New Riders.

Schachter, S., & Singer, J. (1962). Cognitive, social, and physiological determinants of emotional state. *Psychological Review, 69,* 379–399.

Silvia, P. J. (2007). *How to write a lot: A practical guide to productive academic writing.* Washington, DC: American Psychological Association.

Skinner, B. F. (1971). *Beyond freedom and dignity.* New York, NY: Hackett.

Snyder, C. R. (1994). *The psychology of hope.* New York, NY: Free Press.

Susskind, J. E. (2008). Limits of PowerPoint's power: Enhancing students' self-efficacy and attitudes but not their behavior. *Computers and Education, 50,* 1228–1239.

Sweller, J., & Chandler, P. (1991). Evidence for cognitive load theory. *Cognition and Instruction, 8,* 351–362.

Taylor, S. E., & Pham, L. B. (1999). The effect of mental simulation on goal-directed performance. *Imagination, Cognition, and Personality, 18,* 253–268.

Waehler, C. A., & Welch, A. A. (1995). Preferences about APA posters. *American Psychologist, 50,* 727.

Weissman, J. (2005). *In the line of fire: How to handle tough questions . . . when it counts.* Upper Saddle River, NJ: Prentice Hall.

Welch, A. A., & Waehler, C. A. (1996). Preferences about APA poster presentations. *Teaching of Psychology, 23,* 42–44.

Wilder, C., & Rotondo, J. (2002). *Point, click and wow! A quick guide to brilliant laptop presentations.* San Francisco, CA: Jossey-Bass/Pfeiffer.

Yerkes, R. M., & Dodson, J. D. (1908). The relation of strength of stimulus to rapidity of habit formation. *Journal of Comparative Neurology and Psychology, 18,* 459–482.

Zajonc, R. B. (1965, July 16). Social facilitation. *Science, 149,* 269–274.

Index

About the Authors

David B. Feldman, PhD, is an assistant professor in the Department of Counseling Psychology at Santa Clara University, Santa Clara, California. His research addresses such topics as hope, meaning, and growth in the face of trauma, serious medical illness, and other highly stressful circumstances. He is a coauthor of *The End-of-Life Handbook: A Compassionate Guide to Connecting With and Caring for a Dying Loved One* and has published and spoken widely on the psychological aspects of chronic and terminal illness.

Paul J. Silvia, PhD, is an associate professor in the Department of Psychology at the University of North Carolina at Greensboro. His research explores the psychology of emotion, particularly the emotion of interest and its role in aesthetic experience. He won the Berlyne Award, an early-career award given by American Psychological Association Division 10 (Society for the Psychology of Aesthetics, Creativity and the Arts) for his research on the psychology of art and creativity. He recently wrote the books *How to Write a Lot: A Practical Guide To Productive Academic Writing* and *Exploring the Psychology of Interest*.